Annalee Mobilitee Dolls

PRICE GUIDE

Larry Koon

First edition/First printing

Copyright ©2002 Larry Koon. All rights reserved. No part of the contents of this book may be reproduced without the written permission of the publisher.

To purchase additional copies of this book, please contact:
Portfolio Press, 130 Wineow Street, Cumberland, MD 21502
877-737-1200

Library of Congress Control Number 2001-135274
ISBN 0-942620-56-9

Design & Production: Tammy S. Blank
Cover dolls (clockwise from top left): P.J. Kid, 1972; Snow Gnome, 1976; Painter on Scaffold, 1961; Boy in the Band, 1963; P.J. Boy, 1957; Patriotic Boy, Sue Coffee exclusive, 2000; Vacationer, 1970; Roger's Dept. Store Girl, 1950s.

Printed and bound in Korea

Annalee Mobilitee Dolls

PRICE GUIDE

Larry Koon

Consulting Expert, Sue Coffee

Portfolio Press

Dedication

I dedicate this book to the memory of

Annalee Davis Thorndike
1915-2002
Founder and creator of Annalee Mobilitee Dolls

Dear Annalee:
I never had the opportunity to meet you and shake your creative hand, but I've learned so many good things about you while writing this guide, and through many of your fans. I dedicate this guide to your memory, and to all the Annalee collectors out there across the land.   *—Larry Koon*

Acknowledgements

First of all, I would like to thank my publishers, Robert Campbell Rowe, Thomas Farrell and Krystyna Poray Goddu, for issuing me a contract for this book. I really appreciate it.

I want to give a very special thank you to Annalee dealer and expert Sue Coffee of Old Lyme, Connecticut, for taking time out from her busy schedule and lending many hours of her valuable time and expertise to this book, verifying the accuracy of all doll sizes and the years the dolls were originally produced by the Annalee Doll Company, and checking all of the values. Thanks for answering many of my phone calls and sending me photos of your Annalee exclusives, Sue. Without your help and knowledge, the book may have never been written.

I also want to thank Richard Rogers of Lauderhill, Florida, for sending me many photos from his Annalee Doll Collection; Sanders & Mock Auction House in Tamworth, New Hampshire, for sending me auction prices realized from the sale of Annalee Dolls to compare with secondary-market dealer prices; June Rogier of the Annalee Doll Company for sending me many catalogs for reference for this guide and Chuck Thorndike, Annalee's son, for working with me on getting this book published.

I especially want to thank the best mother in the world, who passed away on June 14, 1998, for putting up with me all those years, since I was twelve years old and trying to write my first book. Really miss you, Mom.

I also want to thank "the world's greatest typist," Beth Plummer of Vincent, Ohio, for typing up many of my written manuscripts. I could not have done all this without your help.

To everyone else who supplied me with other bits of information I needed for this price guide, I just want to say you're all the greatest people in the world.   *—Larry Koon*

Contents

©ADM

Introduction

I am very happy to present this up-to-date price guide to more than 2,500 Annalee Mobilitee dolls produced from 1950 through 2001 and sold recently on the secondary market, either at auction or by dealers. The prices in this guide represent many hours of research effort that began with in-depth interviews with Annalee doll experts, secondary-market dealers and auctioneers around the country. I gathered, scanned and compared hundreds of dealer and auction prices to compile the listings in this book.

You will notice that on many of the listings certain pieces of information, such as original edition size, or original retail price, are marked as N/A—meaning not available. June Rogier of the marketing department at Annalee Mobilitee Dolls, reports that none of the production records from the earliest years of the company's existence were saved, due primarily to the small scale of the company's production in those early years. Since Annalee Thorndike began her company by working at the kitchen table, and then expanded into a small cottage industry, no records were kept of the original production numbers or retail prices. In fact, the first price list was not produced until about 1954, and the first full-color product catalog was not published until 1972. Like many small company owners, Annalee and Chip Thorndike were primarily concerned, during their first years of operation, with making their products quickly enough to meet their sales needs. The notion of preserving records for future collectors probably never entered their minds. Collectors who are familiar with the first three volumes of the price guides to Annalee Dolls published in the late 1980s (White Face Publishing) will note that these books are also missing the information on edition sizes and retail prices of early pieces.

Good luck to all of you in buying and selling your collections, whether you choose to do so privately, through secondary market dealers or auction houses. Any collectors who have information to share, or questions to ask, may write me at: P.O. Box 808, Belpre, Ohio 45714.

A Brief History of Annalee Mobilitee Dolls

This postcard from the 1960s shows Annalee Thorndike with some of the company's dolls from that period.

A youthful hobby was the foundation of Annalee Mobilitee Dolls. As a young girl growing up in Concord, New Hampshire, in the 1930s, Barbara Annalee Davis spent many hours creating puppets and dolls and putting on puppet shows with a girlfriend. When her friend went off to college, Annalee turned to making dolls as a way of making a livelihood. The League of New Hampshire Craftsmen had just been formed and this was Annalee's first sales outlet. She priced her dolls at $1.50 each. Eventually she expanded her sales to shops in Boston, where she lived for a short time. Having been brought up in a creative home, with an artistically inclined mother and aunt, Annalee continued to try to perfect her dolls, spending hours working at her artistic skills. She often practiced drawing faces by looking into a mirror and sketching what she saw.

In 1941, Annalee put aside her dollmaking to marry Charles "Chip" Thorndike of Boston. The couple settled in Meredith, New Hampshire, near the shore of Lake Winnipesaukee and started a poultry farm. As a sideline, Chip also sold used auto parts. By the early 1950s, however, the poultry market had become a faltering one, and the couple decided that Annalee would return to dollmaking. They would try their hand at selling the dolls. They set up their business at the kitchen table, where Annalee worked, while Chip went door-to-door selling the dolls she crafted. Eventually they hired a small staff to help, some of who worked at the house with Annalee, while others worked out of their own homes.

From the start the dolls were made from felt and stuffed with cotton batting, with Annalee hand-painting the faces and putting together the dolls. Before long, though, Chip designed an internal wire frame for her pieces, which allowed them to be posed. His innovation gave the dolls their famous "mobilitee." Their posability led to demand for window and advertising displays. The New Hampshire Department of Vacation Travel and Development gave them a large commission for a diorama with more than 150 dolls to be placed in the New Hampshire Tourist Information Office at 30 Rockefeller Center in New York City. The dolls were successful enough that the Thorndikes were able to give up the failing poultry business altogether and concentrate on dolls. In 1954 the company created the first price list and photo sheet, and in

1955 the Thorndikes incorporated their company. Before the 1950s had ended, Annalee Mobilitee Dolls could be found in gift shops, florists, and department stores, which both sold the dolls and used them for displays. Single dolls were priced at $7 and up; larger groups commanded as much as $200. By 1960, the dolls were being sold in forty states, Canada and Puerto Rico.

The Thorndike home in Meredith remained the focal point of the business, but the dolls quickly outgrew the available space. In 1964 the first factory building, known as the Parkersburg, was built on the grounds. By now the line was famous for its Santas, bunnies and the Annalee Mouse. The company was asked to create a large Rhode Island Red Rooster by the State of New Hampshire for display in the Eastern States Exposition. In 1971 the company opened Annalee's Workshop, which is now called Annalee's Gift Shop, and in 1972 they published the first full-color catalog. New creatures introduced in the mid-1970s included the first bear and the first Halloween mouse. Annalee Mobilitee Dolls, which often depicted various holidays, became especially popular as holiday displays in homes and retail businesses. Eventually two-thirds of the company's line was devoted to Christmas-related items. In 1974 the Thorndikes were honored as the New Hampshire Small Business of the Year.

The 1980s were a decade of tremendous growth for the company, by then firmly established as a thriving and successful enterprise with a solid history. The number of employees topped three hundred; expanded sales led to showrooms in major gift markets in New York City and other cities. An article in the November/December 1987 issue of *Dolls* magazine reported that more than two-thirds of the employees were actively engaged in the manufacture of the dolls. "The faces are now done by a technique the company invented, which is a closely guarded secret," explained writer Stephen Gardner in the story. "Each face is individually hand-

The sun pin has long been a core piece in the Annalee Mobilitee Dolls collection, appearing almost every year in the catalog. A special edition of the Sun Pin, with an orange-red background, was included with Doll Society membership kits until the year 2000. The sun pin is one of two corporate logos (the other is the Elf face) that are used in advertising and promotion. Chuck and Karen Thorndike use the sun pins as goodwill ambassadors, passing them out to people they meet in their travels.

brushed and goes through five inspections before being released for sale. There have not been many stylistic changes over the years, but experienced collectors have noted that the company has steadily improved such things as the quality of the clothing, and has added refinements and details which were not present in earlier models."

In 1983, in response to collectors' interest in both the history of Annalee and the collectability of the dolls, a museum was established and the Annalee Doll Society was founded. (For more detailed information on the museum and society, see pages 9 and 11.) The society held its first annual members barbecue and auction in 1984, in Meredith, drawing visitors from all around the country. In an attempt to respond to collectors' need for more information about the value of their older dolls, the company published a three-volume set of guidebooks in 1988 (through White Face Publishing). Another honorary milestone came in 1989, when the Thorndikes traveled to the White House and participated in the unveiling of the Spirit of '76 tableau by then Chief of Staff, John Sununu.

A second trip to the White House came in 1991, when the family presented the Desert Storm mice, in commemoration of the Gulf War, to General Colin Powell, and had a surprise meeting with President Bush. Further demand for the dolls led to the opening of the Annalee North Gift Shop in North Conway, New Hampshire, that year. The following year, 1992, the Thorndikes were again honored when they received the Entrepreneur of the Year award in Light Manufacturing. Innovations in the doll line continued, with 1995 seeing the introduction of the three-inch dolls known as the Itsie Series.

In the second half of the 1990s, Annalee Mobilitee Dolls continued to receive state awards for the employment opportunities it provided. The company was named Employer of the Year for the State of New Hampshire for 1996 by the International Association of Personnel in Employment Security, and placed fourth at the national level.

Annalee Mobilitee Dolls has always created special commissions for local and national groups and companies, such as an edition of 1,000 dolls they created in 1987 for the New Hampshire State Police on the occasion of their fiftieth anniversary. Of particular interest to collectors are the one-of-a-kind and limited-edition pieces created for the Walt Disney World Doll & Teddy Bear Conventions from 1992-1996. These pieces were:

♦ 1992: 10-inch Sailor Bear (one-of-a-kind); 7-inch Sailboard Kid (limited edition)
♦ 1993: 10-inch Rough & Ready Teddy (one-of-a-kind); 7-inch Hawaiian Kid (limited edition)
♦ 1994: 18-inch Scottish Bear (one-of-a-kind); 10-inch Scottish Bear (limited edition)
♦ 1995: 18-inch Lotus Blossom Bear (one-of-a-kind); Chip the Fishing Bear (limited edition)
♦ 1996: 18-inch Bear Masterson Cowboy Bear (one-of-a-kind); 10-inch Indian Chief (limited edition)

In 1998, at the age of eighty-three, Annalee announced her retirement. She turned the leadership of the company over to her son, Chuck Thorndike, who had been involved in the company for many years, and had served as president since the mid-1990s. Her other son, Townsend, preceeded his brother as president. Chip Thorndike is also officially retired from the company, but he continues to be involved with the family business he and Annalee founded and nurtured.

Annalee Davis Thorndike died in Concord, New Hampshire, on April 7, 2002. Her and Chip's spirit and influence live on in the enduring appeal of the Annalee Mobilitee Dolls.

The Annalee Doll Society

When doll collecting exploded in the 1970s and 1980s, it became clear to companies that they should form organizations to attract and educate their most avid customers. Since 1983, the Annalee Doll Society, the nation's largest club devoted to collecting and enjoying Annalee Dolls, has helped keep people across the country informed and entertained. The Society holds annual events, issues members-only special dolls and publishes a quarterly magazine, which keeps members abreast of new lines and releases.

The Society boasts members in forty-five states, Canada and Puerto Rico and has attracted growing crowds to its annual social events since the first auction was held in 1984. Society members from as far away as Alaska regularly make a point of visiting the fall auctions, held at venues throughout the country. Society members receive a subscription to *The Collector*. Published mid-month in January, April and July, the magazine highlights new releases, company news and special mailings for members-only discounts. Announcements for upcoming social events and auctions keep members in-the-know. The magazine also provides the opportunity for members to submit pictures of their own Annalee collections and displays.

Members also receive a seven-inch Logo Kid (each is limited to a year's production) and have had the opportunity in the past to purchase other members-only figures from series such as the Folk Heroes (ten inches), Great American Eras (ten inches), Annalee Animals (eight inches), Annalee's Dolls of the World (seven inches) and Annalee's Collector Kids (seven inches). The first Logo Kid doll was introduced in 1985, and a new one has appeared each year. (Effective with the 2002 release—Mother's Little Helper—these are now referred to by the company as Membership Gifts rather than Logo Kids). Below are the Logo Kids produced as of 2002:

1985-1986	Milk & Cookies
1986-1987	Sweetheart
1987-1988	Naughty
1988-1989	Raincoat
1989-1990	Christmas Morning
1990-1991	Reading
1991-1992	Clown
1992-1993	Back to School
1993-1994	Ice Cream
1994-1995	Dress-Up Santa
1995-1996	Goin' Fishin'
1996-1997	Little Mae Flowers
1997-1998	Tea For Two?
1998-1999	15th Anniversary Kid
1999-2000	Mending My Teddy
2000-2001	Precious Cargo
2001-2002	Mother's Little Helper

The Doll Society also sponsors annual socials and members-only auctions. A members-only auction held in 1980 attracted a whopping 2,000 enthusiasts. The first Summer Social Auction was held in 1984 in Meredith, New Hampshire, attracting 450 members who bid on sixty-one dolls. Since then the number of attendees has grown dramatically, and fall conventions and auctions have been held in locations as diverse as Hershey, Pennsylvania; Williamsburg, Virginia; Columbus, Ohio; and Hollywood, California. From 1980 to 1998, Wayne Mock of Sanders and Mock Auction House in Tamworth, New Hampshire, conducted Doll Society auctions, at which they hammered down pieces for as high as $6,500 for a 1950's 26-inch special order piece designed for Roger's Department Store. Since 1998, the auction duties have been supervised by George S. Foster III of The Complete Auction Service. (See page 12 for more information on the auctioneers.)

Exclusive releases also commemorate Doll Society events. These dolls, available only to members, are issued for one weekend only each year. Through 2001, the event dolls include:

1994	10-inch Red Coat with Cannon (edition of 1,500)
1995	10-inch Tennessee Fiddler (edition of about 350)
1996	10-inch Colonial Candlemaker Woman (edition of approximately 285)
1997	10-inch Harlequin Elf (edition size not available)
1998	7-inch Pirate Elf (edition size not available)
1999	10-inch Southern Belle (edition of 150)
2000	Castle in the Clouds Bear (edition size not available)
2001	7-inch Meredith Mouse (edition of 250) , 7-inch Engineer Mouse (edition of 287), and 10-inch Positioning Pal (edition of 200)

Membership in the Annalee Doll Society is $32.95 per year (July 1 to June 30) and includes the 7-inch Membership Gift (Logo Kid) doll of the year, a subscription to *The Collector*, a felt gingerbread pin and magnet, an enamel lapel pin with date of membership, membership card, and invitations to members-only events and auctions. (Note: The Annalee Doll Society will transition to a calendar year beginning January 2003, when it becomes the Annalee Club.) To join, see any authorized Annalee Doll retailer, visit www.annalee.com, or call (800) 433-6557.

The Annalee Doll Museum

Established in 1983 in Meredith, New Hampshire, the Annalee Doll Museum houses an impressive collection of more than seventy years of Annalee dolls. Set amidst picnic areas and wooded hills, a facade replica of Annalee Thorndike's childhood home at 113 Centre Street in Concord, New Hampshire, is the visitors' first sight. Upon entering, museum-goers learn the history of the Annalee Doll Company and Annalee's own life story, that of an artist and early female entrepreneur who created a company that thrives to this day.

The museum curates more than 1,500 dolls and displays more than 500 at any given time. The earliest Annalee doll on display dates to 1934, and dolls from every subsequent decade are on display, including rare examples of early Santas, Elves, Bunnies and Mice. Unique display and special-order dolls are showcased, and examples of the changes to the Annalee line help collectors learn about their own dolls.

The museum is open from Memorial Day weekend through the Columbus Day weekend. Call 1-800-433-6557 for hours and directions, or visit www.annalee.com.

Identification of the Dolls

This 1957 Santa is approximately 12 inches high (see page 16). Compare this piece to the Santas produced over the decades, and shown throughout this book, to see how the body patterns and materials have changed over the years.

Identifying a doll's age accurately is a matter of expertise and experience, but there are a few general tips for narrowing down an approximate date. Much more detailed information can be found on the company's web site and in issues of the Annalee Doll Society's quarterly magazine, *The Collector*.

I. Tags

♦ 1930s-1940s: Most of Annalee's earliest dolls had white tags of woven fabric, with straight edges and the word "Annalee" printed or sewn on them in black block letters. Other early dolls had tags that said simply "NH" on them in black handwriting, while yet another version of the tag was light or dark green satin with the word "Annalee" woven in script. The tag manufacturer's name "Cash" also appears on the side of these tags.

♦ 1950s: The tags during this first decade of production were either white woven fabric, or white satin, bearing the word "Annalee" in a red script. Some of the tags included the words "Pat. Pending" (patent pending) or a second line indicating "MEREDITH, N.H" in red block letters. In the late 1950s a © was added to the tag.

♦ 1960s: The white woven tag with red embroidered lettering continued to be used, but the copyright © and registration ® marks began to appear regularly on the tags. The year of copyright registration was also added, which indicates only the year the design was copyrighted and not the year it was actually produced. For example, a doll from the late 1960s might have a tag reading: U.S.A. Annalee ® © 1963//Mobilitee Doll Inc. ® Meredith, N.H.

♦ 1970s: Many of the tags in this decade were white satin with red embroidered letters. Verbiage varied widely during the 1970s, but usually included the same elements of the tags from the 1960s. In 1974, a green folded paper hang tag, with string attached, was added to the dolls as well. In 1976 the company began printing the doll's contents on the back of the tag.

♦ 1980s: The company began making its own tags in 1980. Sometime during the decade the logo head was added to the tags and in 1987, the actual year of production of the individual piece (two numbers preceded by an apostrophe, i.e., '87) was added to the sewn-on tag, In 1988 the green hang tag was changed to a beige tag with blue letters.

♦ 1990s: In the 1990s, the company returned to using the white tag with red embroidered lettering. Tags continued to feature the logo head and two-numbered date of production. Annalee Doll Society members-only pieces made in the 1990s bear special tags. In 1992, the tag had yellow embroidered text on blue satin-like material, with the Doll Society logo, along with the current year, printed on the front. In 1993-94, the colors of the Doll Society tag changed to green lettering on white, and remained those colors for the next several years, although the length of the tags varied over the years. In 1995 bar code beige hang tags with black lettering were added to the dolls. In 1997, specialty hang tags were developed for limited editions and exclusives.

♦ In 1999 the company returned to using only one sewn-in white tag with red embroidered lettering.

COLLECTOR'S NOTE: A doll that has Annalee's signature on its tag increases in value by at least $300, and sometimes more at auction.

II. Head Shapes

Annalee's earliest dolls, made before the company came into existence, had a flat spherical-shaped head with a felt-wrapped neck. This style of head continued to be used when the company first began making dolls and was maintained throughout the 1950s.

In the 1960s, the heads took on a pear-like shape. The neck was no longer separate, but was formed as part of the body.

This pear-like shape has evolved slightly over the decades, but has remained generally the same. The neck has continued to be made as part of the body.

III. Hair Material
    1934-1963: yarn
    1960-1963: feather
    1963-present: synthetic fur

IV. Fabric
The Annalee Doll Company used a new Christmas and spring fabric every year, so some dolls can be dated by their fabric. A specific guide to fabric dates can be found on the company's web site.

Information & Buying Resources

A. Web Site
The Annalee Mobilitee Dolls web site holds a wealth of information for beginning and experienced collectors (www.annalee.com). From an extensive biography of Annalee Davis Thorndike herself and a detailed company history to identification help through dated tag and fabric descriptions to catalog archives, the site is an excellent first step for anyone looking to learn more about these dolls. It also includes the standard information on retailers (organized by state), new releases and special events related to Annalee Mobilitee Dolls.

B. Secondary Market Dealers

Sue Coffee, Old Lyme, Connecticut
Authority and secondary-market dealer Sue Coffee has been collecting Annalee Mobilitee Dolls since 1988; her collection now numbers in the thousands, from Annalee's earliest creations in the late 1930s to current pieces. It wasn't long before her passionate expertise turned into a full-fledged business of buying and selling Annalee Dolls on the secondary market. Sue also appraises Annalee Dolls, and serves as a consultant to publications such as this book, Collector's Information Bureau and *Collectors Mart* magazine. She has presented seminars on the subject, and has appeared on the cable television program, "Personal FX: The Collectibles Show."

Since January 2000, Sue has also worked with the Annalee Doll Company in designing pieces sold exclusively by her, which have been featured on the Annalee web site, as well as in *The Collector* magazines. Collectors interested in buying, selling or appraisal of their pieces may contact Sue via her web site: www.suecoffee.com or at the following address: Sue Coffee, 10 Saunders Hollow Road, Old Lyme, Connecticut 06371; (860) 434-5641.

Richard Rogers, Lauderhill, Florida
Richard Rogers is a long-time collector, dealer and senior consulting expert for Annalee Mobilitee dolls, specializing in the

pieces of the 1950s and 1960s. His love of Annalee dolls began in 1966 when he and his grandmother, a New York City seamstress, began collecting and appreciating the fine handiwork of the dolls. A long-time friend of Annalee Thorndike, Richard has been appraising collectors' Annalee dolls for twenty years, and conducts an annual fall auction of high-quality examples in Mystic, Connecticut. Collectors interested in buying, selling or appraisal of their pieces may contact Richard at 4921 NW 65th Ave., Lauderhill, Florida 33319; 954-747-9570; or e-mail rubydolls@aol.com.

C. Auctioneers

Sanders & Mock Auctions

Sanders & Mock Auctions of Tamworth, New Hampshire have been in existence for more than thirty years, selling primarily antiques and fine art, as well as handling commercial liquidations and real estate.

In 1980, Sanders & Mock Auctions began working with the Annalee Doll Company to value their dolls, including those in the Annalee Museum. Wayne Mock, auctioneer, believed the only way to determine the real secondary value of Annalee Dolls, for both insurance and sale, was to hold a series of auctions of Annalee Dolls. He was thus instrumental in coordinating the first Annalee Doll Society auctions.

The first auction was held in 1982 and attracted more than 2,000 collectors from all over the country. Collectors brought with them a wide array of older dolls, artist proofs and one-of-a-kind dolls from the factory. For the next fifteen years, Sanders & Mock conducted at least one sale a year at the Annalee Doll Factory. From 1990 to 1997, the auction house also conducted sales at every Annalee fall convention held in various locations around the country, including Hershey, Pennsylvania, Nashville, Tennessee and Williamsburg, Virginia.

In 1998, the Annalee Doll auctions moved from the Doll Factory in Meredith, New Hampshire, to the Sanders and Mock auction gallery in Chocorua, New Hampshire, where two more Annalee Doll Society auctions were held. These were the last Annalee Summer Social and fall convention auctions conducted by Sanders and Mock.

Having become a leading auction house for Annalee dolls through their official dealings with the Annalee Doll Company, Sanders and Mock also conducted three Annalee in-house sales per year through 2000. Auctions included the sale of early, rare and highly collectible dolls from the 1930s and later, special order dolls, one-of-a-kinds, display dolls and dolls autographed by Annalee herself.

In December, 2001, auctioneer Wayne Mock announced the closure of the company's Chocorua gallery and his semi-retirement. Sanders and Mock Auctions no longer holds public auctions. Collectors may contact Sanders and Mock Auctions at P.O. Box 37, Tamworth, New Hampshire, 03886; (603) 323-8749.

The Complete Auction Service

Auctioneer George S. Foster, III, of The Complete Auction Service has been conducting auctions for the Annalee Doll Company since 1999. He has been conducting auctions and appraisals for more than twenty-five years, specializing in estates, business liquidations, special collections and dolls. With crowds of up to 250 bidders and 70 to 250 Annalee dolls to choose from at each auction, George Foster and his company have clearly maintained the energy of the Summer Social Auction events, as well as other Annalee doll auctions each year. Bids also continue to rise, and George reports a number of high-end bids each year ranging from $2,500 to nearly $7,000.

Collectors may contact The Complete Auction Service, George S. Foster III, CAI, Professional Auctioneer and Appraiser, 386 Suncook Valley Highway, Epsom, New Hampshire 03234-4243; (603) 736-9240; gsfoster3@ aol.com.

D. Annalee Gift Shop

Located a short walk from the Annalee Doll Museum on the grounds of the Annalee Doll Company facilities, Annalee's Country Gift and Christmas Shop is a recently expanded gift shop open all year. It carries the entire current line of Annalee dolls, and may be the only store where collectors can see the full product line, and select the dolls they want. From time to time, unique Annalee Doll products are available at the shop, including dolls with regional themes and short-run samples. In addition, the expanded shop now offers regional gifts, food products and accessories from throughout New England, plus garden decorations, candies and creative holiday gift ideas.

The shop is open daily from 9 a.m. to 5 p.m., except Easter, Thanksgiving, Christmas and New Year's Day. Call (800) 433-6557 or (603) 279-6542 for directions and to order. Visit the gift shop at www.annaleegiftshop.com.

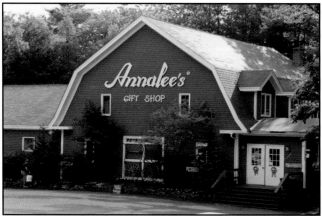

1950s

1957 — A 7-inch Baby Skier came with feather or yarn hair. It wears a ski jacket, baggy ski pants and ski hat. The doll comes in various colors. $500-$1,000 (signed by Annalee).

1950's – This 26-inch Roger's Dept Store Girl was made for a Manchester, New Hampshire department store in the late 1950's. It has wide eyes, smiling face, blonde hair, and wears the original dark brown brim hat, black coat, with large white button at top of coat. $6,500 (in a 1996 auction, signed by Annalee).

1956 – A 10-inch Square Dancing Pair. The boy dancer has black yarn hair, wearing hand-laced leather shoes with linoleum soles. The girl dancer wears a square dancer dress, with petticoat. $1,500.

Year Introduced	Size (Inches)	Doll	Edition Size	Year Retired	Issue Price	Value
1950's	9 In.	Choir Boy**	N/A	N/A	N/A	$1,000
1950's	10 In.	Boy & Girl Skiers**	N/A	N/A	$15.00	$2,500
1950's	10 In.	Frogman (Girl Diver)**	N/A	N/A	$9.95	$3,800
1950's	10 In.	Girl Golfer**	N/A	1950	N/A	$650
1950's	20 In.	Boy & Girl Calypso Dancers**	N/A	N/A	N/A	$2,000
1950's	10 In.	Girl Water Skier**	N/A	N/A	$9.95	$2,500
1954	10 In.	Christmas Elf**	N/A	N/A	$2.50	$1,750
1954	10 In.	Boy Skier **	N/A	N/A	$5.99	$1,000
1954	10 In.	Country Girl**	N/A	1954	$8.95	$2,000
1954	10 In.	Elf	N/A	1954	N/A	$300
1954	10 In.	Saks Fifth Avenue Skier**	50	N/A	$9.95	$2,000
1954	10 In.	Spring Doll**	N/A	N/A	$9.95	$2,000
1955	5 In.	Sno Bunny Child	N/A	N/A	$2.95	$300
1955	7 In.	Boy Skier**	N/A	1955	$10.95	$1,000
1955	10 In.	Bathing Boy**	N/A	N/A	$7.95	$1,050
1955	10 In.	Boy Building Boat	N/A	N/A	$9.95	$525
1955	10 In.	Fisherman & Girl in Boat**	N/A	N/A	N/A	$3,000
1955	10 In.	Boy Skier**	N/A	N/A	$10.95	$2,050
1955	10 In.	Boy Swimmer**	N/A	N/A	N/A	$1,500
1956	5 In.	Sno Bunny Child	N/A	N/A	$2.95	$200
1956	7 In.	Baby Angel w/Feather Hair**	N/A	1957	$3.95	$595
1956	10 In.	Baby Angel**	N/A	1957	$5.95	$600
1956	10 In.	Bathing Boy**	N/A	N/A	$6.95	$850
1956	10 In.	Bathing Girl**	N/A	N/A	$6.95	$850
1956	10 In.	Boy Building Boat**	N/A	N/A	$8.95	$1,200
1956	10 In.	Country Girl**	N/A	N/A	$8.95	$2,800
1956	10 In.	Fishing Girl**	N/A	N/A	N/A	$900
1956	10 In.	Santa on Skis**	N/A	N/A	$10.95	$1,250
1956	10 In.	Skier w/Leg in Cast**	N/A	N/A	$15.00	$3,300
1956	10 In.	Square Dancers	N/A	N/A	$59.95	$1,500
1956	10 In.	Water Skier Boy**	N/A	N/A	$7.85	$2,500
1956	10 In.	Water Skier Girl**	N/A	N/A	$7.85	$2,500
1956	12 In.	Santa w/Stocking	N/A	N/A	N/A	$150-$400
1957	10 In.	Boy Building Boat**	N/A	N/A	N/A	$1,000
1957	10 In.	Boy & Girl In Boat**	N/A	N/A	$17.50	$2,000
1957	10 In.	Boy Skier**	N/A	N/A	$15.95	$1,000
1957	10 In.	Boy Square Dancer**	N/A	N/A	$9.95	$900
1957	10 In.	Boy w/Straw hat	N/A	N/A	N/A	$525
1957	10 In.	Casualty Ski Group**	N/A	N/A	$34.95	$3,150
1957	10 In.	Casualty Toboggan Group**	N/A	N/A	$34.95	$1,250
1957	10 In.	Easter Holiday Doll**	N/A	N/A	$9.95	$1,500
1957	10 In.	Elf w/Musical Instrument**	N/A	N/A	$4.00	$1,000
1957	10 In.	Fishing Girl w/Frog on Line**	N/A	N/A	$6.95	$1,100
1957	10 In.	Fisherman & Girl in Boat**	N/A	N/A	$9.95	$1,300
1957	10 In.	Fourth of July Doll**	N/A	N/A	$9.95	$1,500
1957	10 In.	Girl Skier**	N/A	N/A	$7.50	$2,500
1957	10 In.	Girl Square Dancer**	N/A	N/A	$9.95	$900
1957	10 In.	Golfer Boy**	N/A	N/A	$11.95	$875
1957	10 In.	Golfer Girl**	N/A	N/A	$11.95	$775
1957	10 In.	Mr. Holly Elf**	N/A	N/A	N/A	$1,650
1957	10 In.	Skier w/Leg in Cast**	N/A	N/A	$34.95	$2,000

** Signed by Annalee

Year Introduced	Size (Inches)	Doll	Edition Size	Year Retired	Issue Price	Value
1957	10 In.	Thanksgiving Doll**	N/A	N/A	$9.95	$1,500
1957	10 In.	Valentine Doll**	N/A	N/A	$9.95	$1,500
1957	12 In.	Santa w/Bean Nose (w/o Signature)	N/A	N/A	$19.95	$400
1957	12 In.	Santa w/Bean Nose**	N/A	N/A	$19.95	$1,000
1958	10 In.	Boy Skier**	N/A	N/A	$15.95	$2,500
1958	10 In.	Boy & Girl Square Dancers	N/A	N/A	$9.95	$950
1958	10 In.	Fishergirl w/Frog on Line	N/A	N/A	$6.95	$900
1959	33 In.	Boy & Girl on Tandem Bike	N/A	N/A	N/A	$3,500
1959	7 In.	Girl Skier**	N/A	N/A	N/A	$1,000
1959	7 In.	Santa w/Fur Trim Suit**	N/A	N/A	$2.95	$225
1959	10 In.	Architect	N/A	N/A	$6.95	$500
1959	10 In.	Architect**	N/A	N/A	$6.95	$850
1959	10 In.	Bathing Girl**	N/A	N/A	$7.95	$1,550
1959	10 In.	Boy & Girl in Fishing Boat**	N/A	N/A	$16.95	$1,000
1959	33 In	Boy & Girl on Bike**	N/A	N/A	$16.95	$1,000
1959	10 In	Boy Golfer**	N/A	N/A	$9.95	$800
1959	10 In.	Boy Square Dancer**	N/A	N/A	$9.95	$900
1959	10 In.	Christmas Elf w/Instrument	N/A	N/A	N/A	$250
1959	10 In.	Dentist**	N/A	N/A	$9.95	$2,000
1959	10 In.	Doctor**	N/A	N/A	$11.95	$2,000
1959	10 In.	Elf w/Instrument**	N/A	N/A	$3.50	$2,000
1959	10 In.	Fisherman & Girl in Boat**	N/A	N/A	$16.95	$2,550
1959	10 In.	Football Player**	N/A	N/A	$9.95	$1,500
1959	10 In.	Football Player Center w/Ball**	N/A	N/A	$11.95	$950
1959	10 In.	Gendarme**	N/A	N/A	$3.95	$85
1959	10 In.	Girl Skier**	N/A	N/A	$9.95	$2,500
1959	10 In.	Girl Square Dancer**	N/A	N/A	$9.95	$900
1959	10 In.	Girl Swimmer**	N/A	N/A	N/A	$1,500
1959	10 In.	Texas Oil Man**	N/A	N/A	$9.95	$1,550
1959	10 In.	Thanksgiving Girl**	N/A	N/A	$9.95	$1,800
1959	10 In.	Woodsprite-Green**	N/A	N/A	$6.95	$425

1956 – 12-inch Santa with Stocking wearing original red fur-trimmed suit and hat. It holds a striped Christmas stocking. $400.

1956 – 18-inch P.J. Boy with red yarn hair, wearing a red striped pajama outfit. (signed by Annalee). $1,000.

1957 – 12-inch Bean Nose Santa with white hair, long white beard, thick mustache, thick eyebrows. A bean was used for the nose. $1,000 (signed by Annalee, sold at a 1994 auction). $400 if unsigned.

1957 – 7-inch P.J. Boy with blonde yarn hair and large eyes. He wears Doctor Dentons' pajamas with feet. $700 (signed by Annalee, sold at a 2000 auction).

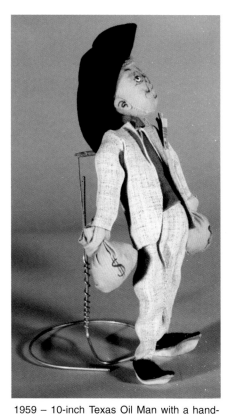

1959 – 10-inch Business Man is dressed in gray dress jacket, gray dress slacks, white shirt and red tie (possibly missing hat). $700.

1959 – 10-inch Dentist wearing a white coat and dark pants. Holding dental drill and dental examining mirror. $600-$2,000 (signed by Annalee).

1959 – 10-inch Texas Oil Man with a hand-painted face, wearing original 10-gallon hat, grayish/tan suit, vest with watch fob, black boots and artificial money in front pocket. Each hand holds a sack labeled "$money$." $4,000 (signed by Annalee, sold at auction).

16

1960s

1962-1963 – This 12-inch Elf is dressed in green. $550 (signed by Annalee, sold at a fall 1994 auction).

1960 – 10-inch Christmas Elf is Red with tinsel. It was also produced in white and green. $200.

1960 – 10-inch Golfer (boy) with visored hat, striped shirt, long pants and golf shoes. It holds a golf club and bag. $500.

Year Introduced	Size (Inches)	Doll	Edition Size	Year Retired	Issue Price	Value
1960's	7 In.	Baby w/Pink Bow**	N/A	N/A	$1.50	$300
1960's	7 In.	Mr. & Mrs. Santa	N/A	N/A	N/A	$150
1960's	7 In.	Mr. & Mrs. Tuckered**	N/A	N/A	N/A	$500
1960's	10 In.	Spring Elf (Pink)	N/A	N/A	N/A	$225
1960's	33 In.	Boy & Girl on Bike**	N/A	N/A	N/A	$4,500
1960	7 In.	Baby Angel w/Feather Hair & Wreath	N/A	N/A	$3.95	$300
1960	7 In.	Baby in Stocking**	N/A	N/A	N/A	$300
1960	7 In.	Elf**	N/A	N/A	N/A	$250
1960	7 In.	Wee Skis (White)	N/A	N/A	$3.95	$175
1960	10 In.	Baby Angel on Cloud	N/A	N/A	$9.95	$400
1960	10 In.	Bathing Girl**	N/A	N/A	$3.95	$1,250
1960	10 In.	Christmas Elf (White)	N/A	N/A	N/A	$175
1960	10 In.	Christmas Elf w/Tinsel	N/A	N/A	N/A	$200
1960	10 In.	Girl Skier**	N/A	N/A	N/A	$1,250
1960	10 In.	Woodsprite w/Broom**	N/A	N/A	N/A	$475
1960	26 In.	Elf w/Bang Hat (Signed by Annalee-94 Summer #102)	N/A	N/A	$9.95	$700
1961	5 In.	Elf w/Tinsel (Green)**	N/A	N/A	N/A	$350
1961	10 In.	Christmas Elf **	N/A	N/A	$2.50	$425
1961	10 In.	Dalmatian Dog	N/A	N/A	N/A	$1,025
1961	10 In.	Spring Elf (Pink)	N/A	N/A	$2.50	$135
1962	7 In.	Baby Angel w/Star on Leg**	N/A	N/A	N/A	$300
1962	10 In.	Boy**	N/A	N/A	$8.99	$900
1962	10 In.	Elf w/Jacket	N/A	N/A	N/A	$200
1962	10 In.	Elf w/Jacket (Signed by Annalee's son Chuck)	N/A	N/A	N/A	$275
1962	10 In.	Skier-Man	N/A	N/A	N/A	$500
1962	26 In.	Bean Nose Santa**	N/A	N/A	$15.95	$750
1963	3 In.	PJ Baby (White)	N/A	N/A	N/A	$250
1963	5 In.	Baby Angel**	N/A	N/A	N/A	$300
1963	5 In.	Baby w/Angel Halo**	N/A	N/A	$2.00	$375
1963	5 In.	Baby w/Santa Hat**	N/A	N/A	$2.50	$300
1963	5 In.	Christmas Elf	N/A	N/A	$3.00	$250
1963	5 In.	Leopard Baby	N/A	N/A	N/A	$250
1963	7 In.	Baby Angel on Cloud**	N/A	N/A	$2.45	$300
1963	7 In.	Baby Angel Powder Puff	N/A	N/A	$1.95	$375
1963	7 In.	Baby w/Green New Hampton Shirt	N/A	N/A	N/A	$475
1963	7 In.	Gnome w/Vest (Green)	N/A	N/A	N/A	$115-$225
1963	7 In.	Gnome w/Vest (Red)	N/A	N/A	N/A	$115-$225
1963	7 In.	Saturday Night Baby**	N/A	N/A	$2.95	$350
1963	7 In.	Skier (Baby Skier)	N/A	N/A	$7.95	$1,250
1963	10 In.	Bathing Boy**	N/A	N/A	$3.95	$1,000
1963	10 In.	Bathing Girl**	N/A	N/A	$3.95	$1,000
1963	10 In.	Boy Building A Boat	N/A	N/A	$9.95	$550
1963	10 In.	Boy & Girl on Tandem Bike	N/A	N/A	$27.95	$575
1963	10 In.	Boy Skier	N/A	N/A	N/A	$185
1963	10 In.	Christmas Elf w/Tinsel	N/A	1963	N/A	$200
1963	10 In.	Elf Skier	N/A	N/A	N/A	$375
1963	10 In.	Elf (Special Order New Hampton Winter Carnival)	N/A	N/A	N/A	$395
1963	10 In.	Elf w/Ski Hat (Green)	N/A	N/A	N/A	$175

** Signed by Annalee

Year Introduced	Size (Inches)	Doll	Edition Size	Year Retired	Issue Price	Value
1963	10 In.	Elf w/Ski Hat (White)	N/A	N/A	N/A	$175
1963	10 In.	Friar (Brown)	N/A	1965	$2.95	$375-$425
1963	10 In.	Girl Water Skier**	N/A	N/A	$5.95	$1,000
1963	10 In.	Go-Go Boy	N/A	N/A	$3.95	$325-$400
1963	10 In.	Go-Go Girl	N/A	N/A	$3.95	$325-$400
1963	10 In.	Ski Girl	N/A	N/A	$8.99	$550
1963	10 In.	Woman Skier	N/A	N/A	N/A	$325
1963	10 In.	Woodsprite (White)	N/A	N/A	$2.49	$300
1963	10 In.	Woodsprite (Red)	N/A	N/A	$2.49	$125
1963	10 In.	Woodsprite (Yellow)**	N/A	N/A	$2.49	$275
1963	10 In.	Workshop Elf	N/A	N/A	N/A	$215
1963	18 In.	Friar	N/A	N/A	$5.00	$400
1963	18 In.	Friar Bottle Cover	N/A	N/A	$3.00	$350
1963	18 In.	Woodsprite	N/A	N/A	N/A	$295
1963	22 In.	Bellhop (Red)**	N/A	N/A	$10.95	$1,750
1963	24 In.	Bellhop**	N/A	N/A	$24.95	$1,200
1963	24 In.	Woodsprite**	N/A	N/A	$5.95	$500
1964	7 In.	Angel in a Basket**	N/A	N/A	$2.00	$300
1964	7 In.	Angel in a Blanket**	N/A	N/A	$2.45	$300
1964	7 In.	Angel w/Lace Outfit	N/A	N/A	N/A	$200
1964	7 In.	Baby w/Blanket**	N/A	N/A	$2.00	$300
1964	7 In.	Bride & Groom Mice**	N/A	N/A	$2.75	$500
1964	7 In.	Christmas Mouse**	N/A	N/A	$3.95	$300
1964	7 In.	Gnome w/Vest (Green)	N/A	N/A	$2.50	$115-$225
1964	7 In.	Gnome w/Vest (Red)	N/A	N/A	$2.50	$115-$225
1964	7 In.	Saturday Nite Angel w/Blanket**	N/A	N/A	$2.50	$350
1964	10 In.	Gendarme**	N/A	N/A	$3.95	$1,000
1964	10 In.	Imperial Skier**	N/A	N/A	$3.95	$400
1964	10 In.	Monk	N/A	N/A	$2.95	$225-$375
1964	10 In.	Robin Hood Elf	N/A	1965	$2.50	$225
1964	12 In.	George & Shelia Bride & Groom Mice**	N/A	N/A	$12.95	$600
1964	18 In.	PJ Boy**	N/A	N/A	$6.95	$450
1964	22 In.	Woodsprite**	N/A	N/A	$5.95	$500
1964	22 In.	Woodsprite**	N/A	N/A	$5.95	$600
1965	7 In.	Green Gnome**	N/A	N/A	N/A	$200
1965	7 In.	Dresden China Babies**	N/A	N/A	$2.50	$400
1965	7 In.	Dumb Bunny**	N/A	N/A	$3.95	$300
1965	7 In.	Eek Peek Squeek Mouse	N/A	N/A	$3.95	$300
1965	7 In.	Lawyer Mouse**	N/A	N/A	$3.95	$200
1965	7 In.	Mr. & Mrs. Santa	N/A	N/A	$5.59	$200
1965	7 In.	Mrs. Santa Mouse w/Muff	N/A	N/A	N/A	$40
1965	10 In.	Back to School Boy & Girl**	N/A	N/A	$19.90	$1,000
1965	10 In.	Fishing Boy**	N/A	N/A	$9.95	$900
1965	10 In.	Fishing Girl**	N/A	N/A	$7.95	$900
1965	10 In.	Monk	N/A	N/A	$3.00	$225
1965	10 In.	Monk w/Christmas Tree Planting	N/A	N/A	$2.95	$300
1965	10 In.	Reindeer	N/A	N/A	$4.95	$500
1965	10 In.	Reindeer w/10 In. Elf**	N/A	1965	$4.95	$625
1965	12 In.	Nipsy Tipsy Hare**	N/A	N/A	$7.50	$1,000
1965	12 In.	Santa	N/A	N/A	$4.95	$125

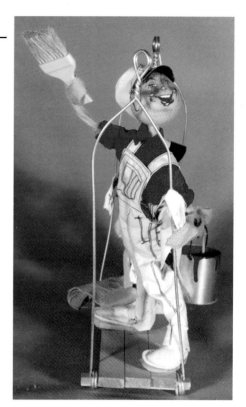

1961 – 10-inch Painter on Scaffold, wearing white coveralls and a painter's hat. It holds a paint can in one hand and paint brush in the other. $1,500 (signed by Annalee).

1963 – 10-inch Boy on Bike, wearing cap, white V-necked shirt, dark shorts and white sneakers. The bike is wire frame, handmade by Chip Thorndike, Annalee's husband. $600 (signed by Annalee, sold at a fall 1994 auction).

1963 – 10-inch Girl on Bike wearing green scarf, striped blouse, red shorts, red shoes. The bike was handmade by Chip Thorndike, Annalee's husband. $600 (signed by Annalee, sold at a fall 1994 auction).

1963 – 10-inch Girl Skier wearing hand-laced ski boots. $1,000 (signed by Annalee).

Year Introduced	Size (Inches)	Doll	Edition Size	Year Retired	Issue Price	Value
1965	18 In.	Santa Kid	N/A	N/A	$6.95	$175
1965	26 In.	Mrs. Santa w/Apron**	N/A	N/A	$14.95	$800
1965	29 In.	Fur Trim Santa**	N/A	N/A	N/A	$475
1966	5 In.	New Hampton School Baby**	300	N/A	N/A	$225
1966	7 In.	Angel White Wings**	N/A	N/A	N/A	$225
1966	7 In.	Bush Beater Baby	N/A	N/A	$2.50	$200
1966	7 In.	Mouse w/Candle**	N/A	N/A		$175
1966	7 In.	Mouse w/Ski Hat	N/A	N/A	N/A	$45
1966	7 In.	Mr. Holly Mouse	N/A	N/A	N/A	$45-$95
1966	7 In.	Mr. Holly & Mrs. Santa Mice	N/A	N/A	N/A	$85
1966	7 In.	Mrs. Santa Mouse (Brown Face)	N/A	N/A	N/A	$125
1966	7 In.	Mrs. Santa Mouse (Grey, flat face)	N/A	N/A	N/A	$100
1966	7 In.	Nightshirt Boy Mouse	N/A	N/A	N/A	$50-$95
1966	10 In.	Boy Skier	N/A	N/A	N/A	$400
1966	10 In.	Central Gas Company Elf**	N/A	N/A	N/A	$175
1966	10 In.	Elf w/Skis & Poles	N/A	N/A	N/A	$195
1966	10 In.	Go-Go Boy & Girl Dancer**	N/A	N/A	$3.95	$550
1966	10 In.	Go-Go Boy Dancer**	N/A	N/A	$3.95	$350
1966	10 In.	Monk in Green Robe	N/A	N/A	N/A	$250
1966	10 In.	Nun	N/A	N/A	N/A	$325
1966	10 In.	Skier on Ski Lift	N/A	N/A	N/A	$400
1966	12 In.	Nurse Mouse	N/A	N/A	N/A	$650
1966	12 In.	Yum-Yum Bunny	N/A	N/A	$9.95	$550
1966	29 In.	Mr. Outdoor Santa	N/A	N/A	$15.00	$125-$225
1966	36 In.	Reindeer-Flat Face	N/A	N/A	N/A	$575
1967	7 In.	Bather Man Ravishing Lovelies	N/A	N/A	N/A	$300
1967	7 In.	Conductor Mouse**	N/A	N/A	$3.95	$300
1967	7 In.	Garden Club Baby**	N/A	N/A	$2.95	$350
1967	7 In.	Gnome w/PJ Suit**	N/A	N/A	$2.95	$200
1967	7 In.	Hangover Mouse	N/A	N/A	$3.95	$50-$225
1967	7 In.	Miguel the Mouse**	N/A	N/A	$3.95	$350
1967	7 In.	Mrs. Holly Mouse	N/A	N/A	$3.95	$150
1967	7 In.	Santa Mouse	N/A	N/A	$3.95	$95-$150
1967	7 In.	Santa w/Toy Bag**	N/A	N/A	$3.95	$150
1967	10 In.	Choir Boy	N/A	1969	$3.00	$225
1967	10 In.	Choir Boy **	N/A	1996	$3.00	$325
1967	10 In.	Elf w/Round Box**	N/A	N/A	$2.50	$350
1967	10 In.	Elf w/Skies & Poles	48	N/A	$2.95	$300
1967	10 In.	Monk	N/A	N/A	$3.00	$200
1967	10 In.	Monk w/Christmas Tree Planting	N/A	N/A	$7.50	$250
1967	10 in.	Monk w/Musical Instrument	N/A	N/A	N/A	$275
1967	10 In.	Surfer Boy	N/A	N/A	$5.95	$300†
1967	10 In.	Surfer Girl	N/A	N/A	$5.95	$350†

†sold at 1994 Auction for $1,200 for the set signed by Annalee

Year Introduced	Size (Inches)	Doll	Edition Size	Year Retired	Issue Price	Value
1967	10 In.	Workshop Elf	N/A	N/A	N/A	$200
1967	12 In.	Cat Sneaky	N/A	1969	$6.95	$375
1967	12 In.	Fancy Nancy Cat Christmas	N/A	N/A	$6.95	$400
1967	12 In.	Gnome w/PJ Suit**	N/A	N/A	$5.95	$400
1967	12 In.	Laura May Cat**	N/A	N/A	$6.95	$400
1967	12 In.	Nightshirt Mouse	N/A	N/A	N/A	$205-$375
1967	12 In.	Mrs. Santa Mouse	N/A	N/A	$9.95	$250-400

** Signed by Annalee

1963 – 10-inch Valentine Couple (Boy and Girl). Valentine Girl wears a red-and-white dress and Mary Jane shawl. Valentine Boy has black hair, and is wearing a red jacket, pants and tie. $1,500 (pair).

1963 – 22-inch Bellhop with bellhop cap, red uniform, gold trim and epaulets. The Bellhop's uniform also come in blue, white, green, yellow, orange and chartreuse. The doll comes with large wire stand. $1,750 (signed by Annalee, sold at a 1996 auction).

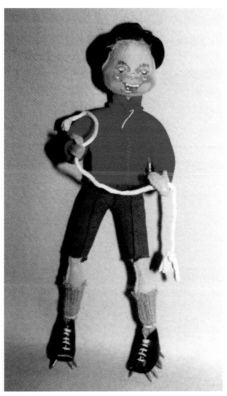

1963 – 10-inch Mountain Climber wearing original red turtleneck shirt, Bermuda shorts and mountain climber shoes. The doll holds a rope. $400 ($750 for an example signed by Annalee and sold at a fall 1994 auction).

1963 – 10-inch Go-Go Girl, wearing a pink-and-white striped Go Go outfit with Go Go boots. $325 (for an example sold at auction).

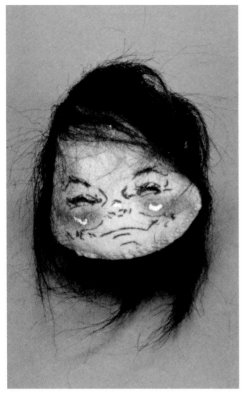

1966-1969 – Hippie (Girl) Headpin with scraggly hair and flowers in hair (not shown). $100.

Year Introduced	Size (Inches)	Doll	Edition Size	Year Retired	Issue Price	Value
1967	12 In.	Yum-Yum Bunny**	N/A	N/A	$9.95	$500
1967	18 In.	Nun**	296	N/A	$7.95	$300
1967	29 In.	Mr. Santa	N/A	N/A	$17.00	$25
1967	36 In.	Christmas Cat**	N/A	N/A	$12	$500
1968	6 In.	Myrtle Turtle**	N/A	N/A	$4.50	$500
1968	7 In.	Baby Angel in Cloud	N/A	N/A	$2.95	$200
1968	7 In.	Baby in Santa Hat	N/A	N/A	$2.95	$200
1968	7 In.	Baby I'm Reading**	N/A	N/A	$2.50	$300
1968	7 In.	Baby in Santa's Hat (Pink)	N/A	N/A	$3.00	$500
1968	7 In.	Baby - Red Hair	N/A	N/A	N/A	$125-$200
1968	7 In.	Baby Vain Jane**	N/A	N/A	$2.50	$300
1968	7 In.	Country Cousin Boy Mouse	N/A	1968	$3.95	$225
1968	7 In.	Country Cousin Girl Mouse	N/A	1968	$3.95	$225
1968	7 In.	Fat Fanny**	N/A	N/A	$5.95	$400
1968	7 In.	Flying Star Angel	N/A	1969	$3.00	$225
1968	7 In.	Mr. Holly Mouse**	N/A	N/A	$3.95	$200
1968	7 In.	Mrs. Claus	N/A	N/A	N/A	$105
1968	7 In.	Mrs. Santa Mouse w/Muff	N/A	N/A	$3.95	$95-$150
1968	7 In.	Mr. & Mrs. Santa Tuckered w/Hot Water Bottle	N/A	N/A	$2.95	$200
1968	7 In.	Nightshirt Boy & Girl Mice**	N/A	N/A	$3.95	$200
1968	7 In.	Painter Mouse (Flat Face) Holds Paint Can & Brush	N/A	N/A	$3.95	$250
1968	8 In.	Elephant (Tubby)	N/A	1968	$7.95	$275

1966 – 12-inch Yum Yum Bunny, in fuchsia, lilac, and orange with different color vests and inner ears. $550 ($850 for an example signed by Annalee and sold at a summer 1994 auction).

1963 – 33-inch Boy & Girl on Bike. The bike originally was handmade by Chip Thorndike, Annalee's husband. $3,500 and $4,500 (signed by Annalee and sold at Annalee Doll Society's 1989 and 1994 auctions).

1968 – 7-inch Mr. and Mrs. Santa are all tuckered out and tucked in with hot water bottles. Mr. Claus has a red flannel outfit. Mrs. Santa has a rosebud print flannel outfit. $200 ($300 for an example signed by Annalee).

1966-1968 – 10-inch Girl Golfer wearing Bermuda shorts and white golf shoes. It originally held a golf club (missing in picture) and bag. $350 ($575 for an example signed by Annalee).

1965 – 10-inch white Reindeer shown with 10-inch Elf. The Reindeer was also available in red or desert sand. $625.

1967 – 10-inch Man with Guitar wearing original striped shirt, long red pants. It is shown with guitar in hand. $1,000 (signed by Annalee, sold at a 1996 auction).

1967 – 10-inch Surfer Boy shown on surfboard. It came in bathing suits of assorted colors. $300. ($525 for an example signed by Annalee sold at a fall 1994 auction).

Year Introduced	Size (Inches)	Doll	Edition Size	Year Retired	Issue Price	Value
1968	10 In.	Boy w/Beach Ball**	N/A	N/A	$5.95	$400
1968	10 In.	Happy Beggar Elf	N/A	N/A	N/A	$150-$275
1968	10 In.	Honkey Donkey (Brown)	N/A	1968	$7.95	$275
1968	10 In.	Horse (Brown w/Hearts)	N/A	N/A	N/A	$425
1968	10 In.	Skinny Minnie Ravishing Lovelies	N/A	N/A	5.95	$300
1968	12 In.	Ice Pack Cat**	N/A	N/A	$6.95	$400
1968	12 In.	Tessie Tar Cat**	N/A	N/A	$6.95	$400
1968	18 In.	Mr. Indoor Santa**	N/A	N/A	$7.50	$200
1968	29 In.	Mrs. Indoor Santa w/Vest & Sack	N/A	N/A	$16.95	$200
1968	36 In.	Reindeer w/Red Nose	N/A	N/A	N/A	$375-$575
1969	4 In.	Pig Bubble Time w/Champagne Glass**	N/A	N/A	$4.95	$300
1969	7 In.	Angel w/Paper Wings (Signed by Annalee 94 Fall #18)	N/A	N/A	$2.95	$275
1969	7 In.	Baby Angel w/Blue Wings**	N/A	N/A	N/A	$300
1969	7 In.	Bunny w/Butterfly on Nose (Yellow)	N/A	N/A	N/A	$125
1969	7 In.	Bunny w/Oversized Carrot**	N/A	N/A	$3.95	$225
1969	7 In.	Carpenter Mouse	N/A	N/A	$3.95	$65
1969	7 In.	Caroler Mouse	N/A	N/A	$4.50	$100
1969	7 In.	Christmas Baby in Hat Boxes**	N/A	N/A	$3.00	$225
1969	7 In.	Plumber Mouse	N/A	N/A	$3.95	$175
1969	7 In.	Santa w/Skies & Poles	N/A	N/A	N/A	$45
1969	7 In.	Ski Mouse	N/A	N/A	$3.95	$85
1969	10 In.	Bride & Groom Frogs Courtin'**	N/A	N/A	$7.95	$450
1969	10 In.	Clown	N/A	N/A	$3.95	$115
1969	10 In.	Nun with Skis	1,551	1969	$3.00	$300
1969	10 In.	Reindeer w/Red Nose	N/A	N/A	$4.95	$100
1969	12 In.	Gnome w/Candy Basket	N/A	1972	$5.95	$225
1969	12 In.	Nightshirt Mouse	N/A	N/A	$9.95	$200
1969	18 In.	Croaker Crosby Frog	N/A	N/A	$10.95	$675
1969	18 In.	Mrs. Claus	N/A	N/A	N/A	$75
1969	18 In.	Santa Kid**	N/A	N/A	$7.50	$350
1969	22 In.	Go-Go Girl Dancer**	N/A	N/A	$9.95	$450
1969	22 In.	Workshop Elf (Red)	N/A	N/A	N/A	$155
1969	25 In.	Country Boy & Girl (Pair)**	69	N/A	$6.95	$750
1969	42 In.	Clown (Pink w/Green)	N/A	N/A	$3.95	$500
1969	42 In.	Frog	30	N/A	$27.95	$700

1967 – 10-inch Tennis Player Girl with black hair, striped scarf around neck and white waffle weave tennis dress. It also has white tennis sneakers and holds an aluminum tennis racquet in one hand. $300.

1968 – 6-inch Turtle with a printed shell. $500 (signed by Annalee).

25

1968 – 10-inch Bathing Beauty from the Ravishing Lovelies Series. $300.

1968 – 7-inch Patches Pam Baby with yarn hair. The unclothed baby came with a felt candle mounted on a felt base. $600 (signed by Annalee, at a fall 1993 auction).

1968 – 10-inch Elephant (Toot) with gray body. It wears a red-and-white striped top hat with a blue felt rim. $295.

1968 – 10-inch Tennis Girl with blonde hair. It wears a striped tennis dress, white felt tennis sneakers with foam sole. One foot is on black wooden base. The doll came with a tennis racket (not shown). $300.

1969 – 7-inch Caroler Boy Mouse with red and white ears, white face and white hair. It wears a green scarf and shoes. $100.

1969 – 7-inch Christmas Baby in Hat Box, wearing only a fur-trimmed Santa hat. The doll is positioned on fluorescent color box. $225.

1969 – 10-inch Bride and Groom. The Groom carries the Bride over the threshold. Both are mounted on an aluminum stand. $600- $700 (Pair) ($950 for an example signed by Annalee and sold at a 1997 auction).

1969 – 10-inch Nun with Skis wearing a white habit, holding skis. It was also available in a black habit. $300.

1970s

1971 – This 10-inch Clown with Mushroom is dressed in its original blue and white outfit. The doll sits next to a mushroom. $350 ($850 for an example signed by Annalee and sold at a fall 1994 auction).

1971 – 7-inch Baby with Bottle has red hair. $125-$150 ($300 for an example signed by Annalee and sold at a fall 1994 auction).

1971 – 10-inch Clown (black-and-white) wearing a black-and-white conical hat, red mittens and white polka-dot clothing. $165 ($300 for an example signed by Annalee and sold at a summer 1994 auction).

Year Introduced	Size (Inches)	Doll	Edition Size	Year Retired	Issue Price	Value
1970	7 In.	Architect Mouse**	205	N/A	$7.00	$225
1970	7 In.	Baby w/Wreath on Head	N/A	N/A	N/A	$125
1970	7 In.	Blue Monkey**	293	N/A	N/A	$400
1970	7 In.	Boxing Mouse**	321	N/A	$3.95	$250
1970	7 In.	Bunny w/Butterfly	1,264	N/A	$5.00	$75
1970	7 In.	Bunny w/Mushroom	340	N/A	$3.95	$300
1970	7 In.	Bunny (Yellow)	3,215	1970	$3.95	$150
1970	7 In.	Carpenter Mouse	307	N/A	$4.00	$75
1970	7 In.	Fireman Mouse	N/A	N/A	$3.95	$90
1970	7 In.	Gnome w/Vest	N/A	N/A	$2.95	$100-$150
1970	7 In.	Going Fishing Mouse	N/A	N/A	$3.95	$95
1970	7 In.	Housewife Mouse	N/A	1970	$11.95	$60
1970	7 In.	Maid Marion Mouse Yr. Issue		1989	$26.95	$50
1970	7 In.	Mailman Mouse (Flat Face) by U.S. Mailbox	541	N/A	$3.95	$250
1970	7 In.	Monkey**	293	N/A	$4.95	$350
1970	7 In.	Nightshirt Girl Mouse	1,518	N/A	$4.00	$75
1970	7 In.	Plumber Mouse**	196	N/A	$4.00	$350
1970	7 In.	Professor Mouse	248	N/A	$4.00	$150
1970/71	7 In.	Santa on Ski-Bob**	836	N/A	$8.50	$250
1970	7 In.	Santa w/Christmas Mushroom	N/A	N/A	$7.00	$200
1970	7 In.	Santa w/10 In. Deer	N/A	1970	$34.95	$125
1970	7 In.	Santa w/10 In. Deer on Christmas Mushroom	N/A	1970	$10.95	$275
1970	7 In.	Sheriff Mouse	N/A	N/A	$3.95	$150
1970	7 In.	Treasure Baby**	N/A	N/A	$4.00	$200
1970	7 In.	Vacationer Boy Mouse	359	N/A	$3.95	$100
1970	10 In.	Casualty Ski Elf w/Arm in Sling	N/A	1972	N/A	$275-$350
1970	10 In.	Casualty Ski Elf w/Crutch & Leg in Cast**	991	1972	$4.50	$350
1970	10 In.	Choir Boy	3,517	1973	$4.00	$150
1970	10 In.	Choir Girl (Red Hair)	7,245	1974	$4.00	$165
1970	10 In.	Clown	2,362	N/A	$4.00	$175
1970	10 In.	Elf Skier	597	N/A	N/A	$250
1970	10 In.	Elf w/Black Hair & Red Outfit	N/A	N/A	N/A	$75
1970	10 In.	Monkey - Chartreuse, Blue or Pink	N/A	N/A	$4.95	$325
1970	10 In.	Monk w/Ski's**	406	N/A	$3.95	$250
1970	10 In.	Nun (Black)	N/A	N/A	N/A	$160
1970	10 In.	Reindeer w/Hat	144	1974	$5.00	$95
1970	10 In.	Santa w/10 In. Deer on Christmas Mushroom**	N/A	1970	$10.95	$450
1970	12 In.	Gnome (Red)	8,475	N/A	$6.95	$75
1970	14 In.	Spring Mushroom**	N/A	N/A	N/A	$450
1970	18 In.	Bunny w/Butterfly	258	N/A	$11.95	$225
1970	18 In.	Bunny (Girl) w/Egg	1,727	N/A	$16.00	$200
1970	18 In.	Clown**	542	N/A	$9.95	$350
1970	18 In.	Gnome w/Apron - Santa's Helper	N/A	1970	$7.95	$325
1970	18 In.	Patchwork Kid**	496	N/A	$7.95	$300
1970	29 In.	Bunny (Girl)	N/A	N/A	$24.95	$300
1970	29 In.	Bunny (White)	N/A	N/A	N/A	$155
1971	5 In.	Gnome w/Candle**	N/A	N/A	$3.00	$350

** Signed by Annalee

Year Introduced	Size (Inches)	Doll	Edition Size	Year Retired	Issue Price	Value
1971	7 In.	Artist Mouse	422	N/A	$4.00	$100
1971	7 In.	Baby Bunting in Basket	195	N/A	$4.00	$100
1971	7 In.	Baby w/Wreath on Head	N/A	1971	N/A	$125-$175
1971	7 In.	Baseball Mouse	553	N/A	$4.00	$75
1971	7 In.	Chef Mouse	614	N/A	$3.95	$75
1971	7 In.	Mouse w/Inner Tube	267	N/A	$4.00	$100
1971	7 In.	Mr. & Mrs. Santa w/Basket	3,403	N/A	$6.00	$100
1971	7 In.	Santa on Ski-Bob w/Sack	1,642	N/A	$5.95	$150
1971	7 In.	Ski Mouse	1,326	N/A	$3.95	$100
1971	7 In.	Snowman	1,197	N/A	$4.00	$125
1971	7 In.	Three Gnomes w/Large Candle**	80	N/A	$12.00	$700
1971	7 In.	Yellow - Kitten**	103	N/A	$4.00	$300
1971	10 In.	Bride & Groom Frogs on Bike**	13	N/A	$18.00	$650
1971	10 In.	Choir Boy	904	1971	$3.95	$150
1971	10 In.	Choir Girl	925	N/A	$3.95	$165
1971	10 In.	Clown (Black & White)	708	N/A	$2.00	$165-$225
1971	10 In.	Elf Skier	1,262	N/A	$3.95	$200
1971	10 In.	Frog w/Instrument	233	N/A	$4.00	$165
1971	10 In.	Nun on Skis	617	N/A	$4.00	$275
1971	10 In.	Reindeer w/Red Nose	1,588	N/A	$5.00	$75-$95
1971	18 In.	Choir Girl	424	N/A	$8.00	$175
1971	18 In.	Frog w/Bass Viola**	224	N/A	$12.00	$750
1971	18 In.	Gnome w/Pajamas	N/A	1972	$8.95	$300
1971	18 In.	Mrs. Santa w/Cardholder	1,563	N/A	$8.00	$110

1971 – 10-inch Monk wearing brown habit and skull cap. It has white hair and beard and holds a brown and white ceramic jug (toothpick holder). $200.

1971 – This 18-inch Gnome with Pajamas has white hair and a white beard. It wears a red body suit with two large buttons and a peaked red cap with a sprig of holly. $300.

1971-1972 – 18-inch Santa's Kid is a blonde baby dressed in red suit with white fur trim. $175 ($250 for an example signed by Annalee).

1972 – 29-inch Mrs. Santa Claus with Wired Skirt for cards (cardholder). It wears a red-and-white striped dress, white cap with holly, white collar and white apron. $150.

1972 – 7-inch Diaper Mouse with gray body and pink ears. The doll holds a sign reading "It's a Boy." $100 (signed by Annalee).

Year Introduced	Size (Inches)	Doll	Edition Size	Year Retired	Issue Price	Value
1971	18 In.	Peter Bunny**	219	N/A	$11.00	$300
1971	18 In.	Santa Fur Kid**	1,191	N/A	$8.00	$300
1971	18 In.	Yellow Boy Bunny w/Butterfly on Nose	N/A	N/A	N/A	$350
1971	18 In.	Yellow Girl Bunny in Turquoise Bandanna w/white Polka Dots	N/A	N/A	N/A	$350
1971	29 In.	Snowman w/Broom	1,075	N/A	$20.00	$300
1971	29 In.	White Bunny w/Carrot	172	N/A	N/A	$300
1971	36 In.	Reindeer w/Two Gnomes	624	N/A	$38.00	$550
1972	7 In.	Ballerina Bunny	4,700	N/A	$4.00	$100
1972	7 In.	Barbecue Mouse	907	N/A	$4.00	$75
1972	7 In.	Bunny w/Bandanna	1,615	N/A	$4.00	$125
1972	7 In.	Christmas Mouse	2,793	N/A	$4.00	$75
1972	7 In.	Diaper Mouse - It's A Boy**	2,293	N/A	$3.95	$100
1972	7 In.	Diaper Mouse - It's A Girl**	2,293	N/A	$3.95	$100
1972	7 In.	Golfer Girl Mouse	1,818	N/A	$4.00	$75-$125
1972	7 In.	Housewife Mouse	1,768	N/A	$4.00	$75
1972	7 In.	Mr. & Mrs. Tuckered	1,187	N/A	$6.00	$125
1972	7 In.	Mrs. Santa w/Apron & Cap	8,867	N/A	$6.00	$75
1972	7 In.	Pregnant Mouse	820	N/A	$6.00	$75-$100
1972	7 In.	Santa w/Mushroom	540	N/A	N/A	$200
1972	7 In.	Yachtsman Mouse	1,130	N/A	$4.00	$120
1972	7 In.	Secretary Mouse	364	N/A	$5.50	$150
1972	8 In.	Elephant	966	1972	$4.00	$275
1972	10 In.	Choir Girl**	2,906	N/A	$4.45	$300
1972	10 In.	Democrat Donkey	861	N/A	$3.95	$300
1972	10 In.	Monk w/Skis & Poles	534	N/A	$4.00	$125
1972	10 In.	Robin Hood Elf	N/A	N/A	$2.00	$125
1972	12 In.	Cat w/Mouse	584	N/A	$12.00	$200
1972	16 In.	Elephant (Republican)**	230	1972	$12.95	$500
1972	18 In.	Gnome w/PJ Suit & Buttons	N/A	N/A	N/A	$185
1972	18 In.	Leprechaun**	1,372	N/A	N/A	$400
1972	18 In.	Mr. Santa w/Sack	850	N/A	N/A	$100
1972	29 In.	Mom Bunny	508	N/A	$35.00	$300
1972	29 In.	Santa w/Cardholder Sack	686	N/A	$25.00	$125
1972	29 In.	Mrs. Snowman w/Cardholder	331	N/A	$19.95	$450
1972	29 In.	Boy Bunny	237	N/A	$25.00	$300
1972	30 In.	Election Donkey**	120	N/A	$24.00	$700
1972	29 In.	Girl Bunny	223	N/A	$25.00	$300
1973	7 In.	Bunny on Box	795	N/A	$4.95	$100
1973	7 In.	Christmas Panda	1,094	1973	$9.00	$325
1973	7 In.	Fireman Mouse	557	N/A	$4.00	$110
1973	7 In.	Football Mouse	944	N/A	$4.00	$75
1973	7 In.	Golfer Mouse	2,108	N/A	$5.00	$75
1973	7 In.	Mr. & Mrs. Santa (Wicker Loveseat)	3,973	N/A	$8.00	$125
1973	7 In.	Painter Mouse	N/A	N/A	$4.00	$100
1973	7 In.	Santa Mailman	3,276	N/A	$5.00	$100-$125
1973	7 In.	Skiing Mouse	2,774	N/A	$4.00	$100
1973	7 In.	Waiter Mouse	N/A	N/A	$4.00	$100
1973	7 In.	White Bunny	1,600	N/A	$6.00	$75
1973	12 In.	Girl Nightshirt Monkey	835	N/A	$8.00	$300

Year Introduced	Size (Inches)	Doll	Edition Size	Year Retired	Issue Price	Value
1973	12 In.	Nightshirt Mouse	122	N/A	$8.00	$125
1973	18 In.	Bear w/Butterfly	384	1973	$10.50	$400
1973	18 In.	Mrs. Santa	3,700	N/A	$9.00	$100
1973	18 In.	Mrs. Santa w/Cardholder	3,900	N/A	$15.00	$100
1973	18 In.	Santa's Helper	2,226	1973	$8.95	$275
1974	7 In.	Artist Mouse	397	N/A	$6.00	$75-$125
1974	7 In.	Black Santa**	1,157	N/A	$5.50	$550
1974	7 In.	Carpenter Mouse	551	N/A	$6.00	$75
1974	7 In.	Cowboy Mouse	394	N/A	$6.00	$100
1974	7 In.	Doctor Mouse	720	N/A	$6.00	$75
1974	7 In.	Hockey Mouse	687	N/A	$5.50	$110
1974	7 In.	Hunter Mouse w/Bird	690	N/A	$5.45	$125
1974	7 In.	Hunter Mouse w/Deer	1,282	N/A	$11.50	$150
1974	7 In.	Painter Mouse (Sloppy)	349	N/A	$5.45	$125
1974	7 In.	Pregnant Mouse	820	N/A	$5.50	$75
1974	7 In.	Seamstress Mouse	387	N/A	$5.50	$80
1974	7 In.	Vacation Boy Mouse	340	N/A	$5.50	$100
1974	10 In.	Fur Trimmed Elf w/Candy Basket	N/A	1974	$5.95	$100
1974	10 In.	Lad & Lass**	453	N/A	N/A	$300
1974	10 In.	Leprechaun w/Sack	8,834	1974	$5.45	$125
1974	10 In.	Willie Wog Goin' Fishing	909	N/A	$6.00	$200
1974	12 In.	Retired Grandma Mouse	1,135	N/A	$14.00	$125
1974	12 In.	Retired Grandpa Mouse	1,103	N/A	$14.00	$125
1974	18 In.	Bob Cratchett & 7 In. Tiny Tim	N/A	1975	N/A	$425
1974	22 In.	Workshop Elf w/Apron (Red)	1,404	1974	$11.00	$175
1974	29 In.	Mrs. Santa w/Cardholder	1,911	N/A	$29.00	$125
1974	42 In.	Willie Wog Frog Going Fishing	223	N/A	$51.95	$900
1975	5 In.	Baby Duck	1,333	N/A	$4.00	$110
1975	7 In.	Beautician Mouse	1,349	N/A	$5.50	$110
1975	7 In.	Bicyclist Mouse	1,561	N/A	$6.00	$110
1975	7 In.	Bouquet Girl Mouse	390	N/A	$5.50	$110
1975	7 In.	Christmas Mouse In Santa's Mittens	3,959	N/A	$5.50	$80
1975	7 In.	Goin' Fishin' Mouse	4,507	N/A	$5.50	$75
1975	7 In.	Housewife Mouse	1,632	N/A	$5.50	$75
1975	7 In.	Pregnant Mouse**	879	N/A	$5.50	$100
1975	7 In.	Retired Grandpa Mouse	793	N/A	$5.50	$75
1975	7 In.	Santa on Bike	5,240	1978	$5.50	$65
1975	7 In.	Santa w/Fur Trim	2,865	1982	$5.50	$30
1975	7 In.	Santa w/Skis & Poles	3,206	1977	$5.50	$85
1975	7 In.	Ski Mouse	5,219	N/A	$5.50	$75
1975	7 In.	Two in Tent Mice	914	N/A	$6.50	$75
1975	8 In.	Rooster	673	N/A	$5.50	$175-$225
1975	10 In.	Caroler Boy	2,056	1976	$5.50	$150
1975	10 In.	Caroler Girl	2,992	N/A	$5.50	$150
1975	10 In.	Drummer Boy	2,913	1975	$5.95	$175
1975	10 In.	Lad & Lass w/Basket**	162	N/A	$12.00	$200
1975	10 In.	Lad on Bicycle**	453	N/A	$6.00	$200
1975	10 In.	Lass w/Balloon	558	N/A	$6.00	$150
1975	10 In.	Reindeer w/Red Nose	4,854	N/A	N/A	$75
1975	10 In.	Reindeer w/Santa Hat	N/A	1982	$17.95	$75
1975	18 In.	Horse	221	1976	$17.00	$275

1972 – 18-inch P.J. Kid. These dolls were also known as Candy Kids or Santa's Kids. This example has blonde hair and wears its original red-and-white striped peaked cap and Dr. Denton's P.J.'s with feet. $200.

1972 – 8-inch Elephant with gray body. It came with a "VOTE" pin (not shown). $250-$275.

1972-1973 – 7-inch Diaper Mouse with gray body, pink ears and painted face. The doll holds a sign reading "It's a girl." $100 (signed by Annalee).

Year Introduced	Size (Inches)	Doll	Edition Size	Year Retired	Issue Price	Value
1975	18 In.	Lad & Lass on Bike	206	N/A	$24.00	$300
1975	18 In.	Lass	224	N/A	$12.00	$225
1975	18 In.	Mrs. Santa Mouse w/Plum Pudding	N/A	N/A	$12.00	$125
1975	18 In.	Yankee Doodle Dandy	N/A	1976	N/A	$250
1975	25 In.	Lass w/Basket of Flowers**	92	1975	$28.95	$400
1975	25 In.	Yankee Doodle on 36 In. Horse**	86	N/A	$76.95	$1,600
1976	7 In.	Angel on Cloud	14,834	1976	$5.50	$30
1976	7 In.	Angel w/Mistletoe	N/A	1993	$19.95	$30
1976	7 In.	Birthday Girl Mouse	732	N/A	$5.50	$75
1976	7 In.	Bunnies - two w/Basket	N/A	1976	$11.00	$125
1976	7 In.	Card Playing Girl Mouse	2,878	N/A	$5.50	$125
1976	7 In.	Colonial Boy Mouse	5,457	1976	$5.50	$125
1976	7 In.	Colonial Girl Mouse	4,430	1976	$5.50	$125
1976	7 In.	Gardener Mouse	1,255	N/A	$5.50	$75-$100
1976	7 In.	Mistletoe Angel	17,540	N/A	$5.50	$30
1976	7 In.	Mr. Holly Mouse	2,774	N/A	$5.50	$75
1976	7 In.	Mrs. Holly Mouse	3,078	N/A	$5.50	$75
1976	7 In.	Nurse Mouse	5,164	N/A	$5.95	$75
1976	8 In.	Rooster	1,094	1977	$5.95	$250
1976	7 In.	Santa & Toy Sack & Sleigh	8,534	1978	$5.50	$45
1976	7 In.	Santa w/Firewood	2,441	1977	$5.95	$55
1976	7 In.	Santa w/Pot Belly Stove	8,639	1982	$5.50	$50
1976	8 In.	Election Elephant**	1,223	1976	N/A	$350
1976	8 In.	White Duck	3,265	N/A	$5.00	$75
1976	10 In.	Girl in Tire Swing	357	N/A	$6.95	$150

1972 – 7-inch Secretary Mouse with orange hair and gray body. The doll wears its original green-and-white striped dress. $150 ($500 for an example signed by Annalee and sold at a fall 1993 auction).

1972 – 30-inch Donkey with tan body and black mane. The doll has a red, white and blue "VOTE" hat and button and red, white and blue striped tie. $650-$750.

Year Introduced	Size (Inches)	Doll	Edition Size	Year Retired	Issue Price	Value
1976	10 In.	Caroler Girl	2,992	1976	$5.50	$150
1976	10 In.	Clown	2,285	N/A	$5.50	$175
1976	10 In.	Colonial Drummer Boy	4,759	1976	$6.00	$225
1976	10 In.	Boy In Tire Swing	N/A	N/A	$7.00	$150-$175
1976	10 In.	Drummer Boy	N/A	N/A	$6.00	$175
1976	10 In.	Elephant	1,223	N/A	$6.00	$300
1976	10 In.	Lass w/Planter Basket**	313	N/A	$7.00	$150
1976	10 In.	Scarecrow	2,346	1976	$5.50	$170
1976	10 In.	Uncle Sam	1,095	N/A	$5.95	$395
1976	10 In.	Vote 76 Donkey	1,202	1976	$6.00	$250-$295
1976	12 In.	Angel on Cloud	2,604	1983	$9.50	$85
1976	12 In.	Colonial Boy & Girl Mouse	1,527	N/A	$27.00	$350
1976	12 In.	Girl Mouse w/Plum Pudding	1,482	N/A	$13.50	$150
1978	12 In.	Gnome	N/A	N/A	$9.50	$135
1976	15 In.	Rooster**	485	1977	$13.50	$400
1976	18 In.	Caroler Girl	1,324	1976	$12.50	$150
1976	18 In.	Choir Boy	N/A	N/A	N/A	$175
1976	18 In.	Clown	916	1976	$13.50	$295
1976	18 In.	Clown**	916	1976	$13.50	$350
1976	18 In.	Easter Parade Boy Bunny	791	N/A	$13.50	$150
1976	18 In.	Elephant**	285	N/A	$16.95	$500
1976	18 In.	Girl Bunny w/Egg	789	N/A	$13.50	$150
1976	18 In.	Scarecrow	916	1976	$13.50	$275
1976	18 In.	Snow Gnome	1,537	1976	$13.50	$300
1976	18 In.	Uncle Sam	245	N/A	$16.95	$750

1973 – 7-inch Mr. Holly Mouse with red body and white head and tail. It wears a red stovepipe hat and lime-green scarf. $200 (signed by Annalee).

1974 – 7-inch Black Santa wearing red fur-trimmed suit and hat, dark green mittens and light green top boots. It carries an over-sized bag. $550 (signed by Annalee, sold at a 1996 auction).

1979 – 7-inch Centerpiece Angel with Candle and Wreath (missing in photo). It wears a white robe, wreath with red candle on head and white felt wings. $100.

35

1975 – 7-inch Ice Skater Mouse with gray body. The doll wears a red jacket with white fur trim. $95.

1975 – 7-inch Pregnant Mouse with gray body. It wears a white dress with floral print. $100 (signed by Annalee).

Year Introduced	Size (Inches)	Doll	Edition Size	Year Retired	Issue Price	Value
1976	18 In.	Vote 76 Donkey**	285	N/A	$16.95	$500
1976	18 In.	Yankee Doodle Dandy	153	N/A	N/A	$250
1976	25 In.	Yankee Doodle Dandy w/30 In. Horse**	41	N/A	$76.95	$800
1976	25 In.	Uncle Sam**	245	N/A	$17.00	$475
1976	29 In.	Scarecrow	256	N/A	$29.95	$500-$700
1976	29 In.	Clown**	466	N/A	$29.95	$500
1976	36 In.	Donkey**	119	N/A	N/A	$650
1976	36 In.	Horse**	27	1976	$48.00	$450
1976	42 In.	Scarecrow	134	1976	$57.95	$1000
1977	7 In.	Baseball Mouse**	1,634	N/A	$6.00	$750
1977	7 In.	Beautician Mouse	1,521	N/A	$5.95	$110
1977	7 In.	Bingo Mouse	1,221	N/A	$6.00	$125
1977	7 In.	Bunny w/Butterfly	2,721	N/A	$6.00	$75
1977	7 In.	Bunny w/Egg	2,442	N/A	$6.00	$75
1977	7 In.	Diet Time Mouse	1,478	1977	$6.00	$125
1977	7 In.	Easter Parade Boy & Girl Bunnies	6,306	N/A	$5.95	$65
1977	7 In.	Groom Mouse	1,211	N/A	$5.95	$75
1977	7 In.	Hobo Mouse	1,004	N/A	$5.95	$125
1977	7 In.	Mr. Nightshirt Mouse	309	N/A	$49.95	$75
1977	7 In.	Santa at Potbelly Stove	9,020	N/A	$5.95	$60-$100
1977	7 In.	Mrs. Santa	N/A	1977	N/A	$45
1977	7 In.	Sweetheart Mouse	3,323	N/A	$6.00	$75
1977	7 In.	Tennis Santa	7,408	1979	$5.95	$50
1977	7 In.	Trick or Treat Mouse	N/A	1989	$16.95	$50
1977	7 In.	Vacation Mouse	1,040	N/A	$6.00	$100
1977	8 In.	Drummer Boy	6,522	N/A	$6.00	$75
1977	8 In.	Rooster	1,642	N/A	$5.95	$250
1977	10 In.	Clown	4,784	N/A	$6.00	$175
1977	10 In.	Leprechaun	N/A	1977	$6.00	$100
1977	10 In.	Scarecrow Multicolored Patchwork Burlap Hat	4,879	1977	$5.95	$225
1977	15 In.	Drummer Boy	N/A	1997	$14.00	$125
1977	15 In.	Purple Rooster**	548	N/A	$5.50	$400
1977	18 In.	Clown**	2,343	N/A	$13.50	$300-$350
1977	18 In.	Easter Parade Boy & Girl Bunny	3,134	1977	$13.50	$250
1977	18 In.	Scarecrow	2,374	N/A	$13.50	$300
1977	22 In.	Jack Frost Elf	2,600	N/A	$12.00	$175
1977	29 In.	Easter Parade Pop Bunny	477	N/A	$34.95	$300
1977	29 In.	Mechanical See Saw Bunny**	N/A	N/A	$300.00	$900
1977	29 In.	Mrs. Santa Mouse w/Muff	571	1977	$49.95	$400
1977	29 In.	Pop Bunny w/Basket	365	N/A	$11.95	$300
1978	7 In.	Airplane Pilot Mouse	2,308	N/A	$6.95	$100
1978	7 In.	Artist Bunny	4,217	N/A	$6.50	$125
1978	7 In.	Bunnies w/Basket (Two)	2,253	N/A	$6.50	$100
1978	7 In.	Card Player Mouse	2,396	N/A	$7.00	$75
1978	7 In.	Doctor Mouse	2,028	N/A	$7.00	$75
1978	7 In.	Fireman Mouse	N/A	N/A	$7.00	$75
1978	7 In.	Gardener Mouse	1,646	N/A	$6.95	$75
1978	7 In.	Girl Golfer Mouse	2,215	N/A	$6.95	$75
1978	7 In.	Groom Mouse	2,952	N/A	$10.00	$75
1978	7 In.	Nightshirt Mouse	6,444	N/A	$8.00	$75

Year Introduced	Size (Inches)	Doll	Edition Size	Year Retired	Issue Price	Value
1978	7 In.	Policeman Mouse	1,189	1978	$6.95	$100
1978	7 In.	Santa w/Deer and Tree	5,813	N/A	$18.45	$125
1978	7 In.	Skateboard Mouse	3,733	N/A	$8.00	$125
1978	7 In.	School Teacher Mouse	2,249	N/A	$6.95	$75
1978	7 In.	Tree Top Angel w/Wreath	8,613	N/A	$6.50	$75
1978	10 In.	Clown	4,020	1978	$6.50	$150
1978	10 In.	Elf w/Planter	1,978	1978	$6.95	$200
1978	10 In.	Leprechaun (Lime Green Body)	N/A	1979	$6.50	$75
1978	10 In.	Pilgrim Boy & Girl	3,461	1978	$7.00	$225/pair
1978	10 In.	Scarecrow (Blue Maroon Patchwork - Red Vest)	N/A	1978	$6.95	$225
1978	10 In.	Snowman	9,701	1979	$6.95	$80
1978	12 In.	Christmas Gnome (Red, White or Green) 10,140		1978	$9.50	$160
1978	18 In.	Boy Bunny w/Basket	2,782	1978	$13.95	$150
1978	18 In.	Candy Girl	1,333	N/A	$11.95	$250
1978	18 In.	Clown**	4,020	1981	$14.00	$300
1978	18 In.	Reindeer w/Saddlebags	5,134	1978	$17.95	$150
1978	18 In.	Scarecrow (Multi-colored Patchwork)	1,844	1978	$13.95	$300
1978	18 In.	Snowman Holding Bird	3,971	1979	$80.00	$125-$150
1978	29 In.	Caroler Mouse	658	N/A	$49.95	$350
1978	29 In.	Easter Parade Mom & Pop Bunnies	529	N/A	$37.00	$450
1978	29 In.	Snowman	1,002	1979	$36.95	$250
1978	36 In.	Reindeer w/Saddlebags	594	N/A	$58.00	$325
1979	4 In.	Boy Pig (White Body)	3,435	1979	$18.50	$65
1979	4 In.	Girl Pig (White Body)	3,719	1979	$18.50	$65
1979	7 In.	Boy Golfer Mouse	2,743	N/A	$8.00	$75
1979	7 In.	C. B. Mouse	1,039	N/A	$7.95	$75
1979	7 In.	C. B. Santa	2,206	N/A	$8.00	$75
1979	7 In.	Carpenter Mouse	2,024	N/A	$7.00	$75
1979	7 In.	Chimney Sweep Mouse	6,331	N/A	$8.00	$75
1979	7 In.	Cross Country Santa w/Skies & Poles	12,556	1981	$7.95	$70
1979	7 In.	Fireman Mouse	1,773	N/A	$7.00	$75
1979	7 In.	Fishing Mouse	3,053	N/A	$7.95	$75
1979	7 In.	Gardener Mouse	1,939	N/A	$7.95	$75
1979	7 In.	Girl Golfer Mouse	2,316	N/A	$8.00	$75
1979	7 In.	Pregnant Mouse	1,856	N/A	$8.00	$75
1979	7 In.	Quilting Mouse	213	1979	$18.00	$160
1979	7 In.	Santa Mouse	12,649	N/A	$8.00	$75
1979	7 In.	Mrs. Santa Mouse w/Holly	12,526	N/A	$8.00	$75
1979	7 In.	Santa w/Mistletoe	11,344	N/A	$8.00	$75
1979	7 In.	Skateboard Mouse	1,821	N/A	$7.95	$125
1979	7 In.	Swimmer Mouse	3,640	N/A	$7.95	$100
1979	7 In.	Teacher Mouse (Boy)	2,041	1979	$7.95	$95
1979	10 In.	Boy Frog	5,642	1981	$8.50	$100
1979	10 In.	Girl Frog	5,970	1980	$8.50	$75
1979	10 In.	Snowman	12,888	N/A	$8.00	$80
1979	12 In.	Caroler Mouse (White)	6,498	1979	$15.95	$125
1979	12 In.	Mrs. Santa Mouse	7,210	N/A	$15.95	$125
1979	12 In.	Nightshirt Mouse w/Candle	5,739	N/A	$15.95	$150
1979	12 In.	Mr. Santa Mouse	5,816	N/A	$15.95	$100

1974 – 18-inch Martha Cratchett with black hair. It wears a long red dress trimmed with white lace, dust cap and apron. It has black boots and holds plum pudding in her hands. $350.

1975 – 18-inch Drummer Boy wearing a blue jacket and blue hat, red leggings and a red-and-white striped scarf. It holds a red, white and blue cardboard drum. $350.

Year Introduced	Size (Inches)	Doll	Edition Size	Year Retired	Issue Price	Value
1979	14 In.	Father Pig	1,500	1979	$19.00	$150
1979	14 In.	Mother Pig	1,807	1979	$19.00	$175
1979	18 In.	Artist Bunny	1,064	N/A	$16.00	$225
1979	18 In.	Girl Frog	2,338	N/A	$18.95	$225
1979	18 In.	Gnome	9,048	1980	$19.95	$225
1979	18 In.	Santa w/Cardholder	N/A	N/A	N/A	$125
1979	29 In.	E. P. Mom & Bunny	662	N/A	$43.00	$200
1979	29 In.	Gnome	1,762	N/A	$48.00	$400
1979	29 In.	Mr. & Mrs. Santa in Motorized Rocking Chair	136	N/A	$400.00	$500
1979	29 In.	Pop Bunny	471	1979	$34.95	$245
1979	29 In.	Snowman	917	N/A	$43.00	$200

1975 – 18-inch Yankee Doodle Dandy with white hair. It wears a blue, visored cap with red feather, blue vest, red-and-white striped suit and blue shoes. Annalee sold this doll riding an 18-inch gray horse with black mane (not shown). At least three examples exist without the horse and show no evidence of having been glued, possibly indicating overruns that were sold in the Annalee gift shop. $250 (without horse).

1976 – 7-inch Colonial Boy Mouse with grey body. It wears a blue tricorne hat, blue jacket and red-and-white striped vest. It holds an American flag. $125.

1976 – 7-inch Colonial Girl Mouse with gray body. It has a red-and-white striped dress and white cap. It holds blue yarn and a needle. $125.

1976 – 10-inch Caroler Boy wearing dark green cap, dark green jacket, bandana-print scarf, red mittens and red leggings. It holds Merry Christmas sheet music. $150.

1976 – 10-inch Caroler Girl wearing her original fur-trimmed hooded red robe. It has a scarf, green mittens and holds Merry Christmas sheet music. $150.

1976 – 10-inch Clown with white hair. The doll wears a conical hat and polka dot navy-and-white clown suit. It has white mittens and large clown feet. $175.

1976 – 10-inch Colonial Drummer Boy wearing blue jacket, blue tricorne hat and red pants. It has a red-and-white scarf and holds a red, white and blue cardboard drum. $225.

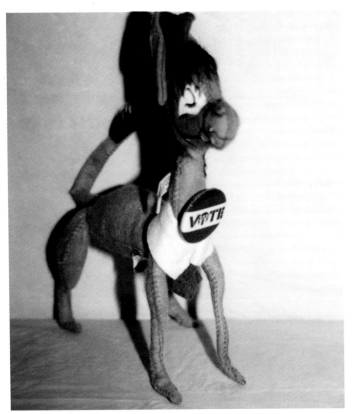

1976 – 10-inch Donkey with tan body. It wears a blue tricorne hat, blue tie and red-and-white striped vest with white collar. The red, white and blue "Vote" button shown did not come with the 1976 Donkey (it is from the 1972 Donkey). $250-$295.

40

1976 – 18 Inch Clown with white hair. The doll wears a conical hat and polka dot navy-and-white clown suit. It has white mittens and large clown feet. $295 (signed by Annalee).

1976 – 18-inch Colonial Drummer Boy wearing blue jacket, blue tricorne hat, red leggings and red-and-white striped scarf. It carries a red, white and blue cardboard drum. $350.

1976 – 18-inch Clown wearing conical hat. Its outfit is red with white polka dots and has white pom poms on the front. $295-$325.

1976 – 10-inch Elephant (Vote '76) with gray body. It wears a red-and-white striped vest, tie and tricorne hat. $295-$325.

1976 – 18-inch Snow Gnome with white hair and beard, and white body. The doll wears a red bandanna-print vest, green sleeveless jacket, and red mittens. $300 ($750 for an example signed by Annalee and sold at a 1996 auction).

1976 – 18-inch Uncle Sam with white hair and beard. It wears a royal blue top hat with white stars, a red-and-white striped suit, a royal blue vest and shoes. It is on a metal stand. $750 ($650 for an example signed by Annalee and sold in a 1989 auction, and $500 for an example signed by Annalee and sold in a 1993 auction).

1976 – (left) 18-inch Elephant "Vote '76" with grey body. It wears a red-and-white striped vest, blue tie and tricorne hat. $500 (signed by Annalee). 1976 – (right) 18-inch Donkey "Vote '76" with tan body. It wears a tricorne hat, blue tie, white collar and red-and-white striped vest. $500 (signed by Annalee).

1976 – 30-inch Elephant (Republican) with gray body. It wears a blue tricorne hat, blue tie, red-and-white striped vest and white collar. $550-$750.

1976 – 29-inch Clown with white hair. Wearing a conical hat and clown suit in red or navy with white polka dots and blue mittens. It has large clown feet. Price $500. (signed by Annalee) ($925 for an example signed by Annalee and sold at a summer 1994 auction).

1976 – 42-inch Clown with red-and-white polka-dot conical hat, red polka-dot clown suit and white gloves. $650-$850.

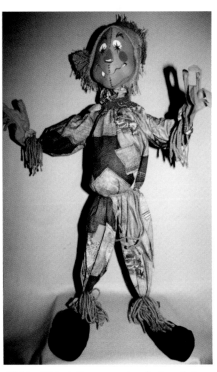

1976 – 10-inch Scarecrow wearing a straw hat and blue denim patchwork print outfit, with neckerchief, mustard gloves and black shoes. $170.

1976 – 18-inch Scarecrow wearing a battered straw hat and blue denim patchwork print outfit, with straw sticking out of wrist and ankles. The doll has a red neckerchief, mustard gloves and black shoes. Its front tooth is showing. $275.

1976 – 29-inch Scarecrow in a battered straw hat and blue denim patchwork print outfit, with straw sticking out of wrist and ankles. It has a red neckerchief, mustard gloves and black shoes. Its front tooth is showing. $500-$700.

1977 – 10-inch Scarecrow wearing a burlap hat and patchwork print outfit tied at the wrists and ankles with brandy colored yarn. It has a red neckerchief, mustard gloves, black shoes and stands on a metal base. Its front tooth is showing. $225.

1976 – 42-inch Scarecrow wearing a peaked burlap hat and blue denim patchwork print outfit, with yarn straw at the wrists, and ankles tied with rope. The doll has a green neckerchief and cotton work gloves. Its front tooth is showing. $1,000.

1977 – 18-inch Scarecrow with a battered straw hat and patchwork print outfit tied at the wrist and ankles. The doll has mustard gloves, black shoes, and stands on a metal base. Its front tooth is showing. $300.

1977 – 48-inch Scarecrow wearing a burlap hat and patchwork print outfit tied at wrist and ankles with straw hanging from them. It has a red neckerchief, white gloves, black shoes. Its front tooth is showing. $875-$1,000.

1978 – 18-inch Scarecrow wearing a black hat with straw sticking out of the crown. The doll wears a red vest and patchwork clothes tied at wrists and ankles with straw protruding from neck. It has mustard gloves. $300.

1977 – 10-inch Clown with white hair and a red nose. It wears a red-and-white striped outfit with flowers and a conical hat. The doll has white mittens and large white clown feet. $175.

1977 – 18-inch Clown (Blue) with white hair and red nose. The doll wears a blue-and-white striped outfit with flowers and a conical hat. It has white mittens and large white clown feet. $300-$350 (signed by Annalee).

1977 – 18-inch Clown (Red) with white hair and red nose. The doll wears a red-and-white striped outfit with flowers and a conical hat. It has white mittens and large white clown feet. $300-$350 (signed by Annalee).

1977 – 8-inch Drummer Boy wearing brown robe and rust hat with holly. It carries a red drum and has rust boots. One toe polks out of boot. $75.

1977 – This is a 7-inch Vacationer Boy Mouse. It has a gray body and wears a Mexican straw hat, and blue, pink or lime green Hawaiian shirt. It holds blue or brown suitcases. $100.

1977 – 7-inch Diet Time Mouse with gray body and white hair, standing on a vertical scale with red cardboard mat. It wears a pink dress with white polka dots. $125 ($200 for an example signed by Annalee and sold at a fall 1995 auction).

1977 – 29-inch Mr. Santa Mouse with gray body. It wears a red fur-trimmed suit. It has green boots and holds a dark-brown burlap sack with two patches (not shown). $425.

1977 – 29-inch Nightshirt Mouse with gray body. It wears a red flannel night-shirt (with a patch) and stocking cap, and features a candleholder. The doll came with red felt slippers and candle. $250.

1977 – 29-inch Mrs. Santa Mouse with Muff. It has a gray body, red fur-trimmed hooded jacket with green boots and a white fur muff sprigged with holly. $400.

1978 – 7-inch Barbecue Mouse. It wears a chef's hat and white apron and holds a frying pan. (Bottom half of frying pan missing in photo.) $75.

1978 – 7-inch Gardener Mouse with gray body. The doll wears blue denim overalls and a red bandana. It holds a hoe and a sheath of straw. $75.

1977 – 48-inch Mrs. Santa Claus wearing a shirt, collar and dust cap. It has a white apron and pantaloons and stands on a red wooden stand. $900.

1978 – 48-inch Mrs. Claus wearing a red-and-white checkered skirt, white apron and pantaloons. Its cap has holly sprigs and it wears black slippers. $900 ($1,450 for an example signed by Annalee and sold at a 1996 auction).

1978 – 48-inch Santa in red flannel. It wears a white fur-trimmed suit and hat, green mittens, and black boots. It carries a green burlap sack with two patches. $400 ($1,450 for an example signed by Annalee and sold at a 1996 auction).

1979 – 7-inch C. B. Mouse with gray body. The doll wears a blue-and-white striped suit and stands on a platform marked "C.B. handle." $75.

1979 – 7-inch Handyman Mouse. It wears blue denim overalls with white stitching and comes with a hammer and/or screwdriver (not shown). $50.

1979 – 7-inch Chimney Sweep Mouse sits on top of a chimney, wearing black hat with red ribbon around the rim of hat. It has black hair, black nose, a red scarf and holds a broom. $75.

1979 – 7-inch Quilting Mouse with gray body. The doll wears a white cap and apron. It was a special order for the Quilt Loft Maplewood Farm, Hillsboro, New Hampshire, which is no longer in business. $160.

1979 – 7-inch Santa at Potbelly Stove wearing a red fur-trimmed suit and hat, dark green mittens and black top boots. $60 to $100 ($375 for an example signed by Annalee and sold at a 1996 auction).

1979 – 7-inch Mr. Teacher Mouse with gray body. It holds a red-framed slate board, with the word "SAT" on it, and came with a pointer (not shown). $95.

1979 – 18-inch Frog with green body. The doll wears green-and-white rompers with pink buttons. $225 ($300 for an example signed by Annalee and sold at a fall 1994 auction).

1978 – 7-inch Policeman Mouse wearing a blue cap, uniform, badge and felt holster. The Policeman Mouse was also produced in 1970-71 with gray or brown body. $100 ($350 for an example signed by Annalee sold at a 1988 auction).

1980s

1981-1982 – This 18-inch Butterfly is shown with a 10-inch Elf. The yellow butterfly has a lime-green elf glued to its wings. The elf wears a white daisy petal cap and bow tie. $200 ($275 for an example signed by Annalee and sold at a summer 1993 auction,$225 for a similar example sold at a fall 1994 auction).

1980 – 7-inch Airplane Pilot Mouse with gray body. The doll wears a tan felt helmet with dark brown felt goggles and a long white scarf. It is holding a single-blade red propeller. $100.

1980 – 7-inch Angel with white felt wings and blonde hair. The doll is unclothed and has a gold or silver halo. $30.

Year Introduced	Size (Inches)	Doll	Edition Size	Year Retired	Issue Price	Value
1980	4 In.	Pig	1,615	1981	$8.50	$75
1980	7 In.	Baby in Bassinet	10,669	N/A	$11.95	$65
1980	7 In.	Backpacker Mouse	1,008	N/A	$10.00	$80
1980	7 In.	Ballerina Bunny	6,013	N/A	$8.95	$75
1980	7 In.	Bride & Groom Mouse	2,418	N/A	$9.50	$125
1980	7 In.	Card Playing Girl Mouse	1,826	N/A	$9.50	$125
1980	7 In.	Chimney Sweep Mouse	4,452	N/A	N/A	$75
1980	7 In.	Disco Boy Mouse	363	N/A	$9.50	$75-$125
1980	7 In.	Disco Girl Mouse	915	N/A	$9.50	$75-$125
1980	7 In.	Fishing Mouse	N/A	N/A	$7.50	$75
1980	7 In.	Gnome	13,238	N/A	$9.50	$75
1980	7 In.	Greenthumb Mouse	1,869	N/A	$9.50	$75
1977	7 In.	Mouse w/Chimney	4,452	N/A	N/A	$75
1980	7 In.	Mouse in Santa Hat	N/A	N/A	N/A	$25
1980	7 In.	Pilot Mouse	2,011	N/A	$9.95	$100
1980	7 In.	Santa w/Stocking	17,665	N/A	$10.95	$40
1980	7 In.	Skating Mouse	3,369	N/A	$10.95	$75
1980	7 In.	Volleyball Mouse	915	N/A	$9.50	$100
1980	7 In.	Witch Mouse on Broom	3,467	1986	$12.50	$55
1980	8 In.	Barbecue Boy Pig w/Frying Pan or Spatula	2,832	1982	$9.95	$125
1980	8 In.	Barbecue Girl Pig	1,240	1981	$10.50	$130
1980	10 In.	Boy Frog	4,185	N/A	$10.00	$100
1980	10 In.	Boy on Raft	1,087	N/A	$28.95	$165-$180
1980	10 In.	Bride & Groom Frog	N/A	1981	$29.95	$300/pr
1980	10 In.	Clown	8,136	1980	$9.50	$110
1980	10 In.	Girl Frog	421	N/A	$10.00	$100
1980	10 In.	Santa Frog w/Toy Bag	7,631	1980	$10.00	$125
1980	12 In.	Witch Mouse on Broom	1,050	1984	$34.95	$125
1980	14 In.	Dragon w/7 In. Bushbeater**	496	1982	$32.95	$450
1980	18 In.	Boy & Girl Frog	2,570	1980	$45.95	$350
1978	18 In.	Country Girl Bunny w/Basket	3,964	N/A	$19.95	$160
1980	18 In.	Clown w/Balloon	3,192	N/A	$25.00	$225
1980	18 In.	Gnome	6,803	N/A	$19.95	$200
1980	18 In.	Santa Frog w/Toy Bag	2,126	1980	$25.00	$300
1980	42 In.	Clown w/Stand	224	N/A	$85.00	$650
1980	42 In.	Santa Frog w/Toy Bag	206	N/A	$100	$500
1981	4 In.	Pig	3,194	N/A	$7.95	$75
1981	5 In.	Miniature Reindeer	9,080	N/A	$8.95	$25
1981	5 In.	Santa w/5 In. Deer	N/A	1984	$19.95	$80
1981	7 In.	Airplane Pilot Mouse	1,910	N/A	$9.95	$95
1981	7 In.	Backpacker Mouse	1,008	N/A	$9.95	$80
1981	7 In.	Baseball Mouse	2,380	N/A	$9.95	$60
1981	7 In.	Boy Monkey w/Banana Trapeze	3,075	1981	$9.95	$175
1981	7 In.	Card Playing Girl Mouse	863	N/A	$9.95	$125
1981	7 In.	Country Boy & Girl Bunnies	7,940	1981	$19.95	$100 Set
1981	7 In.	Cross Country Ski Santa	5,180	N/A	$9.95	$60
1981	7 In.	Escort Fox	1,397	N/A	$12.50	$175
1981	7 In.	Foxy Lady	N/A	N/A	$12.50	$175
1981	7 In.	Ice Skater Mouse	1,429	N/A	$10.00	$75
1981	7 In.	I'm Late Bunny (Special Order)**	100	1981	N/A	$375-$475

** Signed by Annalee

Year Introduced	Size (Inches)	Doll	Edition Size	Year Retired	Issue Price	Value
1981	7 In.	Jogger Mouse	1,783	N/A	$9.95	$75
1981	7 In.	Naughty Angel	12,359	1986	$10.95	$60
1981	7 In.	Nurse Mouse	3,222	N/A	$9.95	$75
1981	7 In.	Santa Fox w/Bag	N/A	1982	$9.95	$195
1981	7 In.	Santa w/Mistletoe	6,592	N/A	$9.95	$75
1981	7 In.	Santa Monkey w/burlap bag	4,606	1981	$9.95	$150
1981	7 In.	Santa w/Pot Belly Stove	8,655	N/A	$11.95	$75
1981	7 In.	Witch Mouse on Broom	4,875	N/A	$12.50	$125
1981	7 In.	Woodchopper Mouse	2,121	N/A	$10.95	$85
1981	8 In.	Ballerina Pig w/Umbrella	N/A	1982	$11.95	$150
1981	8 In.	Boy & Girl Barbecue Pig	3,854	N/A	$10.95	$285
1981	8 In.	Barbecue Girl Pig	2,596	N/A	$9.95	$140
1981	10 In.	Ballooning Santa	1,737	N/A	$39.95	$175
1981	10 In.	Boy on Raft	830	N/A	$28.95	$165
1981	10 In.	Bride & Groom Frog (set)	1,239	N/A	$15.00	$300
1981	10 In.	Clown	6,479	1981	$9.95	$110
1981	10 In.	Elf on Butterfly	1,625	N/A	$24.95	$200
1981	10 In.	Girl Frog	2,044	1981	$9.95	$95
1981	10 In.	Jack Frost Elf w/5 In. Snowflake	5,950	1981	$12.50	$135
1981	10 In.	Workshop Elf	5,553	1983	$9.95	$75
1981	12 In.	Boy Monkey on Banana Trapeze	1,800	1981	$23.95	$300
1981	12 In.	Girl Monkey w/Trapeze	857	N/A	$23.95	$300
1981	12 In.	Pilgrim Boy & Girl Mice	N/A	1989	$47.90	$175
1981	12 In.	Santa Monkey	1,800	1981	$23.95	$275
1981	12 In.	Witch Mouse on Broom	1,049	N/A	$34.95	$125
1981	14 In.	Dragon w/Bushboy	1,257	N/A	$28.95	$300
1981	18 In.	Boy on Sled	3,333	N/A	$24.95	$150
1981	18 In.	Butterfly w/10 In. Elf	2,517	1982	$27.95	$200
1981	18 In.	Cat w/7 In. Mouse & Mistletoe	18,995	1988	$31.95	$170
1981	18 In.	Clown	2,742	1981	$24.95	$225
1981	18 In.	Country Boy Bunny w/Carrot	1,988	1981	$23.95	$150
1981	18 In.	Escort Fox	N/A	N/A	$28.50	$325
1981	18 In.	Foxy Lady	N/A	N/A	$28.50	$325
1981	18 In.	Girl Frog	666	N/A	$23.95	$175
1981	18 In.	Lady & Escort Fox	N/A	1981	$57.95	$650
1981	18 In.	Monk w/Jug	494	N/A	$23.95	$165
1981	18 In.	Santa Fox w/Bag	N/A	1982	$14.50	$275
1981	18 In.	Santa w/Reindeer	3,282	1981	$52.00	$100
1981	18 In.	Workshop Santa	5,422	1990	$44.00	$65
1981	18 In.	Workshop Santa (Animated)	N/A	N/A	$119.95	$275
1981	22 In.	Giraffe w/10 In. Elf	1,377	1982	$36.95	$500
1981	22 In.	Sun Mobile	3,003	1985	$36.95	$225
1981	29 In.	Dragon w/Bushboy**	75	N/A	$69.95	$750
1981	48 In.	Clown	N/A	1981	N/A	$625
1982	3 In.	Butterfly Pick	N/A	1982	N/A	$130
1982	3 In.	Santa w/Gift Box & Card	N/A	1985	$12.95	$45
1982	5 In.	Dragon w/Bushboy	1,066	1982	$17.95	$225
1982	5 In.	Mrs. Santa w/Gift Box	7,566	1985	$10.95	$50
1982	5 In.	Santa w/Bag	5,421	1985	$9.95	$55
1982	5 In.	Santa w/Deer	N/A	N/A	$19.95	$80
1982	5 In.	Santa w/5 In. Deer & Sleigh	1,451	1984	$52.95	$250

1980 – 7-inch Treetop Angel with Halo wearing a white robe. The robe has white netting overlay and collar. The doll includes a gold halo and white felt wings. $40.

1981 – 7-inch Centerpiece Angel with Candle and Wreath wearing a white robe. The doll features a wreath and candle on its head, white felt wings and a white collar. $50.

1981 – 4-inch Pig with tan-colored body and pink ears. The doll has a napkin around its neck. $75 ($250 for an example signed by Annalee and sold at a fall 1994 auction).

Year Introduced	Size (Inches)	Doll	Edition Size	Year Retired	Issue Price	Value
1982	5 In.	Santa w/Stove	3,825	1984	$11.50	$80
1982	7 In.	Angel w/Instrument	N/A	1996	$21.95	$35
1982	7 In.	Angel w/Teardrop	3,092	N/A	$11.95	$110
1982	7 In.	Baby in Bassinet	2,049	N/A	$13.95	$125
1982	7 In.	Ballerina Bunny	4,179	N/A	$11.95	$80
1982	7 In.	Bride Mouse	3,681	N/A	$11.95	$45
1982	7 In.	Cheerleader Mouse	3,441	N/A	$10.95	$45
1982	7 In.	Chef Mouse	3,776	1989	$12.95	$60
1982	7 In.	Cowboy Mouse	3,776	N/A	$12.95	$100
1982	7 In.	Easter Parade Boy Bunny	7,108	N/A	$11.95	$50
1982	7 In.	Equestrienne Mouse	867	1983	$12.50	$125
1982	7 In.	Football Mouse	2,164	N/A	$10.95	$75
1982	7 In.	Girl Tennis Mouse	2,443	N/A	$10.95	$50
1982	7 In.	Graduate Boy Mouse	4,971	N/A	$11.95	$50
1982	7 In.	Graduate Girl Mouse	3,563	N/A	$10.95	$50
1982	7 In.	Groom Mouse	3,406	N/A	$10.95	$45
1982	7 In.	I'm a Ten Baby	2,159	1982	$12.50	$75
1982	7 In.	Mouse w/Strawberry	4,041	1995	$11.95	$50
1982	7 In.	Mr. A. M. Mouse	2,184	N/A	$11.95	$100
1982	7 In.	Quilting Mouse	3,547	1983	$12.00	$25
1982	7 In.	Santa Fox w/Bag	3,622	N/A	$12.95	$175
1982	7 In.	Santa in Sleigh	16,796	1986	$12.95	$40
1982	7 In.	Santa Wreath Center Piece	1,150	N/A	$18.95	$50
1982	7 In.	Sweetheart Mouse	4,110	N/A	$10.95	$50
1982	7 In.	Windsurfer Mouse	4,114	N/A	$13.95	$100
1982	7 In.	Witch Mouse on Broom	2,798	N/A	$12.50	$50
1982	7 In.	Woodchopper Mouse	1,910	N/A	$11.95	$85
1982	8 In.	Ballerina Pig	1,058	N/A	$12.95	$150-$175
1982	8 In.	Boy Barbeque Pig	1,044	N/A	$11.95	$135
1982	8 In.	Caroler Girl	4,687	1986	$12.95	$40
1982	10 In.	Annalee Artist Doll	600	N/A	$295.00	$800
1982	10 In.	Elf on Butterfly	882	N/A	N/A	$200
1982	10 In.	Jack Frost w/Snowflake	2,289	1982	$13.50	$135
1982	10 In.	Monk w/Jug	6,968	N/A	$13.00	$75
1982	12 In.	Boy Skunk	935	1982	$27.95	$150
1979	12 In.	Drummer Boy	4,473	N/A	$28.95	$25
1982	12 In.	Duck w/Kerchief	5,861	N/A	$24.95	$85
1982	12 In.	Girl Skunk	936	1982	$27.95	$175
1982	12 In.	Nightshirt Mouse	2,319	N/A	$25.95	$125
1982	12 In.	Pilgrim Boy Mouse	2,151	N/A	$27.95	$125
1982	12 In.	Pilgrim Girl Mouse	2,017	N/A	$27.95	$85
1982	12 In.	Skunk w/Snowball	1,304	1982	$27.95	$250
1982	16 In.	Caroler Girl	1,952	1984	$27.95	$95
1982	16 In.	Monk w/Jug	N/A	N/A	$27.95	$95
1982	18 In.	Sledding Girl	3,281	N/A	N/A	$100
1982	18 In.	Girl P.J. Kid	5,389	N/A	$25.50	$125
1982	18 In.	Santa Fox w/Bag	1,499	N/A	$29.95	$275
1982	22 In.	Christmas Giraffe w/10" Elf	448	N/A	$43.95	$375
1982	22 In.	Sun Mobile	838	N/A	$29.95	$200-$225
1982	29 In.	Country Girl Bunny	N/A	1982	$61.95	$300
1982	29 In.	Easter Parade Girl Bunny	N/A	1982	$65.95	$225

1984 – 8-inch Monk with Jug with white hair and white beard. It wears a brown skull cap and habit with a white rope belt. The doll carries a white and brown jug. $80.

Year Introduced	Size (Inches)	Doll	Edition Size	Year Retired	Issue Price	Value
1982	29 In.	E. P. Boy & Girl Bunny	N/A	1982	$132.00	$550
1982	36 In.	Reindeer**	N/A	N/A	N/A	$300
1982	48 In.	Country Boy Bunny	186	N/A	$189.95	$900
1982	48 In.	Country Girl Bunny w/Basket	176	N/A	$189.95	$900
1983	3 In.	P.J. Kid	2,360	1983	$10.95	$175
1983	5 In.	Bunny on Music Box	N/A	N/A	$29.95	$225
1983	5 In.	Country Girl Bunny	5,163	N/A	N/A	$75
1983	5 In.	Dragon w/Wings & Baby	199	N/A	$22.50	$325
1983	5 In.	Duckling in Hat	N/A	1984	$10.95	$50
1983	5 In.	Easter Parade Boy Duck	5,133	N/A	$11.95	$50
1983	5 In.	Easter Parade Girl Duck	5,577	N/A	$11.95	$50
1983	5 In.	Floppy Ear Boy Bunny w/Basket	6,099	1984	$11.50	$100
1983	5 In.	Mr. & Mrs. Tuckered	4,600	1983	$22.95	$175
1983	5 In.	Sweetheart Duck	1,530	N/A	$11.50	$65
1983	7 In.	Angel w/Instrument	N/A	N/A	$29.95	$30
1983	7 In.	Cheerleader Mouse	2,025	N/A	$11.95	$50
1983	7 In.	Classic Snowman	N/A	N/A	N/A	$65
1983	7 In.	Country Boy Bunny w/Butterfly	N/A	N/A	$12.50	$60
1983	7 In.	Country Girl Bunny w/Flower Pot	N/A	1983	$10.50	$50
1983	7 In.	Cowboy Mouse	1,794	N/A	$12.95	$100
1983	7 In.	Cowgirl Mouse	1,517	N/A	$12.95	$100
1983	7 In.	E. P. Boy Bunny	N/A	N/A	$12.50	$50
1983	7 In.	E. P. Girl Bunny	N/A	N/A	$12.50	$50
1983	7 In.	Equestrian Mouse	1,283	N/A	$12.95	$125
1983	7 In.	Fishing Boy	2,764	N/A	$12.95	$75
1983	7 In.	Floppy Ear Bunny w/Butterfly	N/A	1983	$12.95	$50
1983	7 In.	Quilting Mouse	2,786	N/A	$11.95	$80
1983	7 In.	Santa at North Pole	N/A	1987	$17.95	$30
1983	7 In.	Santa w/White Felt Moon	N/A	1984	$25.00	$100
1983	7 In.	Snowman Holding Broom	15,980	1983	$12.95	$75
1983	7 In.	Windsurfer Mouse	2,352	N/A	$13.95	$100
1983	8 In.	Monk w/Jug	3,502	1984	$13.95	$80
1983	10 In.	Ballooning Elves	7,395	N/A	$59.95	$300
1983	10 In.	Scarecrow (Blue/White Ticking w/Red Vest)	N/A	1984	$12.95	$125
1983	10 In.	Workshop Elf	5,018	N/A	$11.95	$75
1983	12 In.	Bride Mouse	854	N/A	$31.95	$150
1983	12 In.	Easter Parade Duck w/Basket	N/A	1986	$28.95	$90
1983	12 In.	Groom Mouse	826	N/A	$31.95	$150
1983	16 In.	Monk w/Jug	N/A	1984	$28.95	$150
1983	18 In.	Classic Snowman	N/A	N/A	N/A	$95
1983	18 In.	Fawn	1,444	N/A	$32.95	$225
1983	18 In.	Gingerbread Boy w/Brown Jacket	5,027	1984	$28.95	$135
1983	18 In.	Girl & Boy w/Sleigh	N/A	1983	$79	$195
1983	18 In.	Scarecrow (Blue, White Ticking w/Red Vest)	2,300	1984	$32.95	$225
1983	18 In.	Sledding Boy	3,075	1984	$29.95	$100
1983	18 In.	Sledding Girl	2,971	1984	$29.95	$100
1983	18 In.	Snowman w/Broom	N/A	1996	$28.95	$60-$80
1983	22 In.	Skating w/Mouse	N/A	N/A	N/A	$75
1983	22 In.	Sun	N/A	N/A	N/A	$200-$225

1982 – 16-inch Monk with Jug wearing brown habit and skull cap. It holds a brown jug with holly. $150 ($525 for an example signed by Annalee and sold in a 1996 auction).

1981 – 7-inch I'm Late Bunny, with white body, white hair and pink ears, was a special order. It wears a yellow-and-black checkered shirt and blue vest. The doll carries a pocket watch. $325 (For examples signed by Annalee and sold at auctions: $450, 1986; $475, 1993; $375, 1995).

1983 – 72-inch Santa wearing a red fur-trimmed suit and hat. It has black boots and belt, green mittens and carries a burlap sack. $3,500 (signed by Annalee, sold at a 2001 auction).

1983 – 7-inch Cheerleader Mouse (Special Order) with a gray body. The doll wears a white shirt and holds a gold megaphone with "Go" inscribed on it. $450 (signed by Annalee and sold at a 1996 auction).

Year Introduced	Size (Inches)	Doll	Edition Size	Year Retired	Issue Price	Value
1983	24 In.	Standing Stork w/Baby	858	1983	$36.95	$150
1983	24 In.	Stork w/Baby	858	N/A	$36.95	$150
1983	29 In.	Country Girl Bunny w/Basket	N/A	1983	$69.95	$300
1983	30 In.	Red Christmas Elf	529	N/A	$54.95	$125
1984	5 In.	Country Bunnies w/Basket	1,110	N/A	N/A	$150
1984	5 In.	Duck in Santa Hat	2,371	N/A	$12.95	$50
1984	5 In.	Easter Parade Boy & Girl Bunny	N/A	1984	$23.95	$195
1984	5 In.	Girl Bunny	2,594	N/A	$11.50	$100
1984	5 In.	Mrs. Santa	3,227	1985	$10.98	$50
1984	5 In.	Pilot Duckling	4,396	1985	$14.95	$65
1984	7 In.	Angel Mouse	2,093	N/A	$14.95	$40
1984	7 In.	Angel on Star	772	1994	$32.95	$225
1984	7 In.	Baseball Kid	2,079	N/A	$15.95	$60
1984	7 In.	Bowling Mouse	1,472	1984	$13.95	$75
1984	7 In.	Boy w/Firecracker	1,893	1984	$19.95	$150
1984	7 In.	Boy w/Kite	N/A	N/A	N/A	$50
1984	7 In.	Boy w/Snowball	6,269	1988	$15.95	$45
1984	7 In.	Bunny	N/A	1985	$14.00	$45
1984	7 In.	Christmas Morning Kid	6,938	1986	$18.95	$45
1984	7 In.	Country Bunnies w/Basket	2,345	N/A	$25.95	$80
1984	7 In.	Country Girl w/Basket	715	N/A	$16.95	$40
1984	7 In.	Cupid In Heart	2,445	N/A	$32.95	$135
1984	7 In.	Cupid Kid	6,808	1985	$14.95	$55
1984	7 In.	Cupid Kid in Hanging Heart	1,667	1985	$19.95	$135
1984	7 In.	Dentist Mouse	2,362	N/A	$14.95	$55
1984	7 In.	Devil Mouse	3,571	N/A	$11.95	$40
1984	7 In.	Easter Parade Boy Bunny	5,989	1984	$12.95	$40
1984	7 In.	Girl on Sled	6,620	1986	$15.95	$50
1984	7 In.	Hockey Player Mouse	1,525	N/A	$5.50	$75
1984	7 In.	Jogger Kid	N/A	N/A	$17.95	$45
1984	7 In.	Mouse w/Presents	N/A	1992	$17.95	$45
1984	7 In.	Mouse w/Strawberry	1,776	N/A	$11.95	$45
1984	7 In.	Mouse w/Wreath	5,492	1984	$12.95	$40
1984	7 In.	Mrs. Retired Mouse	1,356	N/A	$13.95	$65
1984	7 In.	Mrs. Santa	N/A	1984	N/A	$40
1984	7 In.	Naughty Angel	4,528	N/A	$14.95	$60
1984	7 In.	Nightshirt Mouse	N/A	N/A	$11.95	$40
1984	7 In.	Pilgrim Mice Set w/Basket	N/A	1992	$44.00	$75
1984	7 In.	Santa on a Moon	2,119	N/A	$25.00	$100
1984	7 In.	Snowball Mouse	N/A	N/A	N/A	$40
1984	7 In.	Snowman w/Pipe	10,023	1992	$14.95	$35
1984	7 In.	Teacher Mouse (Girl)	5,064	N/A	$13.95	$80
1984	7 In.	Two Bunnies w/Bushel Basket	2,339	N/A	$25.95	$90
1984	7 In.	Valentine Bunny**	5,602	1985	$13.95	$75
1984	8 In.	Monk w/Jug	3,502	N/A	$17.95	$80
1984	10 In.	Aerobic Girl	4,875	1985	$19.95	$50
1984	10 In.	Bride & Groom	1,993	1985	$62.95	$150
1984	10 In.	Bride & Groom**	1,993	1985	$62.95	$700
1984	10 In.	Caroler Boy	6,998	1986	$15.95	$45
1984	10 In.	Clown	6,383	1984	$14.00	$75
1984	10 In.	Downhill Skier	3,535	N/A	$31.95	$100

Year Introduced	Size (Inches)	Doll	Edition Size	Year Retired	Issue Price	Value
1984	10 In.	Gingerbread Man	4,615	1984	$15.95	$55
1984	10 In.	Groom	685	N/A	$31.95	$90
1984	10 In.	Johnny Appleseed w/Dome	1,500	N/A	$80.00	$425
1984	10 In.	Robin Hood w/Dome	1,500	N/A	$89.95	$325-$450
1984	10 In.	Scarecrow	3,008	N/A	$15.95	$125
1984	10 In.	Skier (Cross Country)	2,714	1986	$31.95	$125
1984	12 In.	Devil Mouse	1,118	1984	$29.95	$175
1984	12 In.	Naughty Angel	1,310	1986	$32.95	$85
1984	12 In.	Tree Top Angel w/Gold Star	2,219	1985	$31.95	$75
1984	16 In.	Monk w/Jug	1,821	N/A	$34.95	$150
1984	18 In.	Aerobic Dancer	622	N/A	$35.95	$125
1984	18 In.	Bear w/Brush	1,392	1984	$39.95	$220
1984	18 In.	Bob Cratchett	1,819	N/A	$49.95	$175
1984	18 In.	Sledding Boy	2,205	N/A	$28.95	$100
1984	18 In.	Candy Boy	1,350	N/A	$29.95	$150
1984	18 In.	Candy Girl	1,333	N/A	$29.95	$150
1984	18 In.	Cardholder Santa (Various Fabrics)	N/A	N/A	N/A	$50
1984	18 In.	Christmas Panda w/Toy Bag	7,427	1986	$39.95	$150
1984	18 In.	Clown (Green & White Polka Dot)	N/A	1984	$32.95	$225
1984	18 In.	Clown (Orange w/White Dots)	1,828	N/A	$32.95	$225
1984	18 In.	Country Boy Bunny	N/A	1984	$39.95	$150
1984	18 In.	Country Girl Bunny w/Basket	1,481	N/A	$39.95	$125
1984	18 In.	Fawn w/Wreath	1,444	N/A	$32.95	$225
1984	18 In.	Gingerbread Boy (Brown Jacket)	1,774	N/A	$28.95	$135
1984	18 In.	Sledding Girl	2,328	N/A	$29.95	$100
1984	18 In.	Martha Cratchett	1,751	N/A	$35.95	$175
1984	18 In.	Monk w/Jug	1,821	N/A	$34.95	$150
1984	18 In.	Scarecrow	1,956	N/A	$32.95	$225
1984	30 In.	Clown	387	N/A	$69.50	$325
1984	30 In.	Monk	432	N/A	$78.95	$400
1984	30 In.	Mrs. Santa w/Cardholder Apron	SU	N/A	N/A	$125
1984	30 In.	Snowgirl w/Muff	685	N/A	$79.50	$525
1984	30 In.	Snowman w/Broom	956	N/A	$79.50	$300
1984	32 In.	Monk w/Garland**	416	N/A	$78.50	$600
1984	48 In.	Snowman	N/A	N/A	$169.95	$1,000
1985	5 In.	E. P. Girl Duckling	N/A	1985	$13.95	$45
1985	5 In.	Easter Parade Boy & Girl Duckling	N/A	1985	$27.95	$55
1985	7 In.	Baseball Kid	1,221	N/A	$16.95	$60
1985	7 In.	Birthday Girl	1,017	N/A	$18.95	$40
1985	7 In.	Boy Bunny w/Carrot	3,273	1985	$14.95	$40
1985	7 In.	Boy Golfer Mouse	2,099	N/A	$14.95	$50
1985	7 In.	Bride & Groom Mice	2,963	N/A	$13.95	$85
1985	7 In.	Country Bunnies w/Candy Jar	N/A	N/A	N/A	$45
1985	7 In.	Cupid Kid	2,875	N/A	$15.50	$125
1985	7 In.	Cupid Kid in Hanging Heart	778	N/A	$32.95	$135
1985	7 In.	Dress up Boy	1,174	N/A	$18.95	$80
1985	7 In.	Dress up Girl	1,536	N/A	$18.95	$80
1985	7 In.	Drummer Boy	8,368	1992	$16.50	$40
1985	7 In.	Get Well Mouse	1,425	N/A	$14.95	$50
1985	7 In.	Girl Tennis Mouse	1,947	N/A	$14.95	$55
1985	7 In.	Graduation Boy Mouse	1,999	N/A	$13.95	$40

1982 – 7-inch Baby in Bassinet dressed in white eyelet lace gown and bonnet. It has a white plastic bassinet trimmed with yellow lace. $125.

1985 – 7-inch Valentine Bunny holding lace-trimmed red felt valentine reading "Be Mine." It wears a red dress with tiny white hearts, white lace trim and a red ribbon in her hair. $75.

1987 – 7-inch Barbecue Mouse. The doll wears a chefs hat, white scarf and red-and-white checkered apron. It holds a hamburger grill. $60.

1985-1986 – 10-inch Baby Bear with Bee with brown body and blonde hair. The doll wears blue fabric overalls. A bumblebee sits on the bear's nose. $95 ($350 for a 1985 example signed by Annalee and sold at a 1988 auction).

Year Introduced	Size (Inches)	Doll	Edition Size	Year Retired	Issue Price	Value
1985	7 In.	Graduation Girl Mouse	2,884	N/A	$13.95	$40
1985	7 In.	Happy Birthday Boy	937	N/A	$18.95	$60
1985	7 In.	Happy Birthday Girl	1,017	N/A	$19.00	$70
1985	7 In.	Hiker Mouse w/Backpack	1,781	1985	$13.95	$65
1985	7 In.	Hockey Player Kid	1,578	N/A	$19.00	$75
1985	7 In.	Jogger Kid	654	N/A	$16.95	$45
1985	7 In.	Kid w/Kite	1,084	1985	$16.95	$50
1985	7 In.	Logo Kid w/Pin	3,562	N/A	N/A	$375
1985	7 In.	Santa w/Gift List & Toy Bag	N/A	1992	$23.95	$25
1985	7 In.	Skiing Kid	N/A	1987	$17.50	$90
1985	7 In.	Valentine Bunny	5,602	N/A	$13.95	$75
1985	10 In.	Aerobic Girl	2,147	N/A	$18.95	$150
1985	10 In.	Annie Oakley (Artist Proof)**	1,500	N/A	$95.00	$395
1985	10 In.	Annie Oakley w/Dome	1,500	N/A	$95.00	$195-$325
1985	10 In.	Bride	318	N/A	$31.95	$90
1985	10 In.	Christmas Panda w/Toy Bag	4,397	1986	$18.95	$65
1985	10 In.	Clown	5,815	1986	$14.95	$75
1985	10 In.	Cross Country Skier	1,150	N/A	$33.50	$115
1985	10 In.	Groom	264	N/A	$31.95	$90
1985	10 In.	Hot Air Balloon w/10 In. Clown	812	1986	$49.95	$150
1985	10 In.	Panda w/Toy Bag	1,904	N/A	$17.95	$85
1985	10 In.	Penguin and Chick	3,000	1985	$30.00	$90-$125
1985	10 In.	Penguin & Chick**	3,000	AP	$29.95	$575
1985	10 In.	Penguin & Chick w/Dome	3,000	N/A	$79.95	$150
1985	10 In.	Reindeer w/Bell	6,398	N/A	$13.95	$40
1985	10 In.	Ski Elf	N/A	1986	$17.95	$85
1985	10 In.	Valentine Panda	N/A	N/A	N/A	$85
1985	12 In.	Drummer Boy	3,745	1992	$31.95	$65
1985	12 In.	Duck w/Raincoat & Umbrella	3,534	1986	$36.95	$100
1985	12 In.	Indian Boy & Girl Mice	N/A	1987	$71.95	$160
1985	12 In.	Jazz Cat w/instrumental French Horn	2,622	1985	$31.95	$160-$195
1985	12 In.	Kid w/Sled	4,707	1986	$31.50	$100
1985	12 In.	Naughty Angel w/Slingshot	1,393	N/A	$34.95	$85
1985	15 In.	Jazz Cat w/Trumpet**	2,622	1985	$31.95	$425
1985	18 In.	Ballerina Bear	19,918	1985	$39.95	$200
1985	18 In.	Bear w/Heart	N/A	1986	$41.95	$150
1985	18 In.	Bear w/Honey Pot & Bee	2,032	1986	$41.50	$175
1985	18 In.	Cat w/Heart	N/A	1986	$35.00	$200
1985	18 In.	Christmas Panda	2,207	N/A	$43.95	$150
1985	18 In.	Country Boy Bunny w/Watering Can	2,355	1988	$44.95	$150
1985	18 In.	Country Boy Bunny w/Wheelbarrow	N/A	1986	$57.00	$150
1985	18 In.	Clown w/Balloon	1,485	1986	$34.95	$200
1985	18 In.	Valentine Cat w/Heart	2,129	1986	$32.95	$225
1985	18 In.	Velour Mr. & Mrs. Santa	N/A	1990	$121.95	$160
1985	22 In.	Sun Mobile	579	N/A	$36.95	$200
1985	60 In.	Christmas Tree Skirt	1,332	N/A	$24.95	$175
1986	3 In.	Clown Ornament	3,369	N/A	$11.95	$55
1986	3 In.	Skier	3,904	1988	$13.95	$55
1986	5 In.	Duck on Sled	7,393	1994	$19.95	$55
1986	5 In.	Duck w/Raincoat & Umbrella	5,029	1986	$18.50	$60
1986	7 In.	Birthday Girl Mouse	3,724	N/A	$14.95	$40

Year Introduced	Size (Inches)	Doll	Edition Size	Year Retired	Issue Price	Value
1986	7 In.	Boating Mouse	2,320	1986	$15.95	$65
1986	7 In.	Boy Bunny w/Carrot	2,949	N/A	$15.50	$40
1986	7 In.	Bunny w/Egg	2,233	N/A	$16.95	$40
1986	7 In.	Bunny w/Sled	N/A	1988	$17.95	$50
1986	7 In.	Cupid Kid in Hot Air Balloon	391	1986	$54.95	$185
1986	7 In.	Indian Girl Mouse w/Papoose	6,992	N/A	$18.50	$45
1986	7 In.	Mouse w/Wheelbarrow	2,037	N/A	$16.95	$75
1986	7 In.	Mr. & Mrs. Victorian Santa	N/A	1988	$19.95	$90
1986	7 In.	Planter Mouse w/Wheelbarrow	N/A	1986	$17.00	$65
1986	7 In.	Skiing Kid	8,057	N/A	$18.50	$75
1986	7 In.	Sweetheart Kid w/Pin	6,271	1986	$17.95	$175-$250
1986	7 In.	Tennis Mouse	1,947	N/A	$15.95	$55
1986	7 In.	Valentine Bunny	N/A	N/A	$14.50	$75
1986	7 In.	Victorian Santa w/Sleigh & Deer	6,820	1988	$43.95	$85
1986	7 In.	Witch Mouse in Pumpkin Balloon	868	N/A	$59.95	$275
1986	10 In.	Baby Bear w/Bee	6,496	1986	$19.50	$350
1986	10 In.	Bear w/Sled	6,081	1989	$26.95	$75
1986	10 In.	Christmas Panda w/Toy Bag	4,397	N/A	$18.95	$85
1986	10 In.	Clown	3,897	N/A	$15.50	$75
1986	10 In.	Elf Skier (Green Outfit)	2,726	1987	$17.95	$125
1986	10 In.	Fishing Bear	2,817	1986	$19.95	$150
1986	10 In.	Girl Bear	4,018	1987	$19.95	$85
1986	10 In.	Hot Air Balloon w/10 In. Clown	2,700	N/A	$17.00	$175
1986	10 In.	Kitten w/Yarn & Basket	3,917	1987	$27.95	$100
1986	10 In.	Mark Twain w/Dome	2,500	N/A	$117.50	$195-$350
1986	10 In.	Unicorn w/Plaque	3,000	1986	$36.95	$110-$125
1986	10 In.	Valentine Panda	1,940	1986	$19.95	$125
1986	12 In.	Naughty Angel w/Slingshot	1,934	1986	$36.95	$75
1986	12 In.	Trick or Treat Halloween Mouse	N/A	1990	$42.95	$85
1986	12 In.	Witch Mouse Holding Trick or Treat Bag	N/A	1990	$42.95	$75
1986	14 In.	Pumpkin (Solid)	N/A	1992	$48.95	$150
1986	14 In.	Pumpkin Balloon w/7 In. Witch Mouse	N/A	1987	$59.95	$300
1986	15 In.	Hobo Cat	2,130	1988	$27.95	$100
1986	18 In.	Country Boy Bunny w/Wheelbarrow	1,224	N/A	$46.95	$150
1986	18 In.	Country Girl Bunny w/Flowers	1,205	N/A	$41.95	$125
1986	18 In.	Clown	1,485	N/A	$36.95	$150
1986	18 In.	Reindeer w/Saddlebags	4,857	1994	$38.95	$95
1986	18 In.	Valentine Cat	1,069	N/A	$34.95	$225
1986	18 In.	Victorian Velour Mr. & Mrs. Santa	N/A	1987	$115.00	$250
1986	18 In.	Victorian Velour Mrs. Santa	2,000	1987	$57.50	$125
1986	30 In.	Boy Bunny w/Wheelbarrow	252	N/A	$119.50	$250
1986	30 In.	Easter Parade Boy & Girl Bunny	N/A	1986	$189.95	$450
1986	48 In.	Velour Santa	410	1988	$269.95	$600-$750
1987	3 In.	Baby in Basket	2,900	1987	$15.00	$100
1987	3 In.	Baby Witch w/Diaper	3,645	1987	$13.95	$100
1987	3 In.	Boy w/Snowball	N/A	1988	$13.95	$45
1987	3 In.	Bride & Groom	1,250	1987	$39.00	$95
1987	3 In.	Cupid in Heart Balloon	1,715	1987	$12.95	$150
1987	3 In.	Cupid Kid	899	N/A	$12.95	$35

1989 – 7-inch Businessman Mouse with tan body. It wears a gray flannel jacket and hat and a red vest with watch chain. The doll carries a black briefcase. $45.

1986 – Artist's proof 10-inch Unicorn with dome, base and brass plaque. The white Unicorn, forelegs reared, stands on a cloud above an aqua felt base. $110 (no base or dome) ($350 for an example signed by Annalee and sold at a 1990 auction; $1,050 for an artist's proof signed by Annalee and sold at a 1986 auction).

1984-1985 – 7-inch Cupid Kid in Hanging Heart with blonde hair and white felt wings. The doll has wooden arrows tipped with red points, an aluminum bow with red yarn strings and a red felt quiver. It is glued in the center of a laced heart. $135 ($375 for an example signed by Annalee and sold at a fall 1994 auction).

1988-1990 – 10-inch Eskimo Bear with brown body. The doll wears a hooded parka with white fur trim and colorful braid trim, light beige felt boots and red mittens. It is on a snow-covered wire stand. $90.

Year Introduced	Size (Inches)	Doll	Edition Size	Year Retired	Issue Price	Value
1987	3 In.	Jack-O-Lantern	N/A	1998	$23.95	$45
1987	3 In.	Witch Kid Baby	3,289	N/A	$13.95	$100
1987	5 In.	Christmas Morning Kid w/3 In. Bear in Box	2,025	1989	$30.45	$65
1987	5 In.	Elf w/Deer	6,700	N/A	$9.95	$35
1987	5 In.	Leprechaun	5,461	1992	$13.50	$30
1987	5 In.	Monk	878	1987	$13.95	$85
1987	7 In.	Baby w/Blanket & Knit Sweater	7,836	1989	$19.95	$50
1987	7 In.	Baby Mouse	2,500	N/A	$13.95	$55
1987	7 In.	Barbecue Mouse	1,798	N/A	$17.95	$60
1987	7 In.	Bicyclist Boy Mouse	1,507	N/A	$19.95	$50
1987	7 In.	Boy on Victorian Sled	N/A	1989	$22.95	$65
1987	7 In.	Bride Mouse	1,801	N/A	$14.50	$45
1987	7 In.	Cupid Mobile	1,487	N/A	$16.95	$65
1987	7 In.	Ghost Kid w/Pumpkin	3,652	1997	$21.95	$65
1987	7 In.	Graduation Boy	2,034	1987	$19.95	$65
1987	7 In.	Graduation Girl	2,438	1987	$19.95	$50
1987	7 In.	Groom Mouse	1,800	N/A	$14.50	$45
1987	7 In.	Hangover Mouse	1,548	1987	$13.95	$175
1987	7 In.	Indian Boy & Indian Girl Mouse	4,500	1996	$17.95	$95
1987	7 In.	Kangaroo w/Plaque	3,000	N/A	$37.50	$100
1987	7 In.	Kid w/Snowball	3,400	N/A	$18.45	$45
1987	7 In.	Naughty Kid w/Pin	11,000	1988	$19.95	$110
1987	7 In.	Pilgrim Kids w/Basket	3,400	1992	$35.95	$75
1987	7 In.	Santa w/Sleigh & One Reindeer	575	1990	$65.95	$120
1987	7 In.	Victorian Mr. & Mrs. Santa	8,160	N/A	$21.95	$100
1987	10 In.	Bear in Nightshirt w/Candle	6,600	1993	$23.95	$60
1987	10 In.	Bear in Velour Santa Suit	N/A	1992	$32.95	$75
1987	10 In.	Bear w/Snowball Knit Hat & Scarf	4,100	1992	$28.95	$60
1987	10 In.	Ben Franklin w/Dome	2,500	N/A	$119.50	$225-$325
1987	10 In.	Bride & Groom Cats	727	1987	$71.95	$275-$325
1987	10 In.	Carrot Balloon w/7 In. Bunny	N/A	1987	$49.95	$150
1987	10 In.	Christmas Goose	N/A	1989	$29.95	$60
1987	10 In.	Clown (Pink and Blue)	2,139	1987	$17.95	$80
1987	10 In.	Collector Santa Trimming Lighted Tree	950	N/A	$129.95	$225
1987	10 In.	Easter Parade Goose	3,343	1988	$29.50	$65
1987	10 In.	Elves (Two w/Tree, Sled & Ax)	2,000	1988	$43.95	$125
1987	10 In.	Fall Elf (Orange, Brown or Moss Green Outfit)	5,000	1989	$13.95	$55
1987	10 In.	Frog in Top Hat w/Tails and Brass Instrument	1,700	1988	$23.95	$60
1987	10 In.	Huck Finn w/Dome	1,200	1988	$102.95	$225
1987	10 In.	Kitten on Sled	3,600	1991	$33.95	$65
1987	10 In.	Kitten w/Knit Mittens	5,550	1992	$30.95	$55
1987	10 In.	Leap Frogs	1,800	1987	$31.95	$95
1987	10 In.	Nativity Set w/Dome & Plaque	1,475	1990	$139.95	$295
1987	10 In.	New Hampshire State Trooper w/Dome	836	1987	$133.95	$225-$500
1987	10 In.	Pumpkin (Medium)	N/A	1987	$34.95	$200

Year Introduced	Size (Inches)	Doll	Edition Size	Year Retired	Issue Price	Value
1987	10 In.	Reindeer w/Santa Hat & Bell	N/A	1995	$15.00	$25-$35
1987	10 In.	Santa Frog w/Toy Bag	2,300	1987	$19.95	$50
1987	10 In.	Frog w/Instrument	2,162	1987	$19.95	$85
1987	10 In.	Ski Elf w/Sweater	5,000	1987	$19.95	$115
1987	10 In.	Spring Elf	5,996	1991	$13.95	$85
1987	10 In.	Stork w/3 In. Baby in Basket	700	1988	$49.95	$110-$140
1987	12 In.	Duck on Sled- Macys Exclusive	300	N/A	N/A	$200
1987	12 In.	Flying Angel w/Instrument	1,325	1987	$36.95	$85
1987	18 In.	Bottle Cover Monk	718	1987	$29.95	$150
1987	18 In.	Cardholder Santa	N/A	N/A	N/A	$85
1987	18 In.	Chef Santa Gingerbread	N/A	1996	$60.95	$110
1987	18 In.	Macys Workshop Santa	N/A	1987	$39.50	$150
1987	18 In.	Mr. & Mrs. Santa in Rocking Chair	N/A	1988	$124.95	$275
1987	18 In.	P. J. Kid	3,100	1987	$33.95	$85
1987	18 In.	P. J. Kid w/2 Christmas Stockings	N/A	1995	$59.95	$95-$115
1987	18 In.	Victorian Country Boy Bunny	1,394	1987	$49.95	$90
1987	18 In.	Victorian Country Girl Bunny (Pair)	1,492	1987	$49.95	$90
1987	18 In.	Victorian Mr. Santa	2,150	1987	$49.95	$125
1987	18 In.	Victorian Mrs. Santa Cardholder	2,000	1987	$49.95	$145
1987	18 In.	Victorian Santa w/Stocking	2,150	1987	$62.50	$145
1987	18 In.	Workshop Santa	980	1987	$35.00	$60
1987	24 In.	Christmas Goose w/Basket	N/A	1989	$55.00	$135
1987	24 In.	Easter Parade Goose	1,647	1988	$49.95	$150
1987	30 In.	Mr. & Mrs. Tuckered	N/A	1991	$292.00	$325
1987	30 In.	Mr. Victorian Santa	450	N/A	$150.00	$250
1987	30 In.	Mrs. Victorian Santa	425	N/A	$150.00	$250
1987	48 In.	Carrot	2,503	1987	$39.95	$200
1988	5 In.	Duck in Egg	6,100	1990	$19.45	$50
1988	5 In.	Owl	3,000	N/A	$37.50	$60
1988	7 In.	Bunny Kid	7,100	1990	$21.95	$55
1988	7 In.	Bunnies on Music Box Maypole	5,602	N/A	$13.95	$300
1988	7 In.	Bunny Trick or Treat Kid	N/A	1991	$25.95	$55
1988	7 In.	Bunny w/Sled	3,050	N/A	$21.95	$50
1988	7 In.	Country Boy Bunny w/Hoe	3,700	1988	$15.95	$35
1988	7 In.	Eskimo Boy	8,150	1989	$22.95	$65
1988	7 In.	Indian Girl	2,250	1988	$23.95	$55
1988	7 In.	Raincoat Kid w/Pin	13,646	1989	$19.95	$75
1988	7 In.	Skeleton Kid	5,072	1991	$21.95	$65
1988	7 In.	Witch Kid w/Nose	4,500	1992	$22.95	$55
1988	8 In.	Boy Turkey (Tan, Brown Body)	N/A	1995	$34.95	$75
1988	10 In.	Artist Bunny	N/A	1989	$31.95	$95
1988	10 In.	Aviator Frog	N/A	1988	$15.95	$45
1988	10 In.	E. P. Boy & Girl Bunny	N/A	1988	$39.95	$70
1988	10 In.	E. P. Girl Pig	3,400	1988	$24.50	$75
1988	10 In.	Eskimo Bear	7,500	1990	$31.95	$90
1988	10 In.	Frog	840	1988	$15.95	$50
1988	10 In.	Huck Finn Folk Hero Series	400	N/A	$102.95	$225
1988	10 In.	Nativity Set (Artist Proof)**	925	AP	$149.95	$800
1988	10 In.	Scrooge w/Plaque	5,650	1990	$89.95	$135-$165
1988	10 In.	Shepherd Boy & Lamb w/Plaque**	1,275	1990	$89.95	$250-$295
1988	10 In.	Sherlock Holmes w/Dome	2,500	N/A	$119.50	$225-$275

1989 – 10-inch Country Boy Bunny with Basket. It has a tan body and wears blue overalls. The doll has a burlap hat and pink-and-white polka dot neckerchief. It holds a basket filled with strawberries, and is on a wire stand with green base. $85.

1989 – 10-inch Country Girl Bunny with Flowers. It has a tan body and a pink dress with white polka dots, white pantaloons and a white bonnet with ribbon. It holds flowers and is on a wire stand with light green base. $85.

1987 – 7-inch Graduate Boy with black hair and wearing a navy cap and gown. The doll has white sneakers, a yellow tassel on cap, and holds a white diploma with blue ribbon. It is on a dark green stand. $65.

1985 – 12-inch Duck with Raincoat and Umbrella. It has a white body and white felt wings, and wears a bright yellow raincoat and hat with black fasteners. The doll holds a black umbrella. $100.

1985 – 60-inch Tree Skirt made of green felt, with a large Santa face stitched on each side. $175 ($350 for an example signed by Annalee and sold at a fall 1994 auction).

Year Introduced	Size (Inches)	Doll	Edition Size	Year Retired	Issue Price	Value
1988	10 In.	St. Nicholas w/Plaque	N/A	1990	$69.95	$100
1988	10 In.	Stork w/3 In. Baby	500	N/A	$49.95	$110-$140
1988	10 In.	Toy Soldier	762	1990	$32.95	$75
1988	12 In.	Turkey (Large)	N/A	1992	$57.95	$125
1988	18 In.	American Couple w/Plaque	750	1988	$169.95	$325
1988	18 In.	Artist Bunny	2,167	1989	$51.95	$120
1988	18 In.	Chef Santa (Animated) Bowl	N/A	1989	$120.00	$300
1988	18 In.	Country Boy & Girl Bunny	N/A	1988	$89.95	$135
1988	18 In.	Country Mother Bunny w/10 In. Baby Bunny	1,800	1989	$65.95	$135
1988	18 In.	Santa w/Gift List & Toy Sack	2,962	1988	$35.95	$50
1988	18 In.	Toy Soldier	4,470	1990	$49.95	$75-$125
1988	18 In.	Workshop Santa (Animated)	N/A	1989	$119.95	$275
1988	30 In.	Victorian Mrs. Santa w/Tray	N/A	N/A	$119.95	$200
1989	3 In.	Santa In Metal Sleigh	N/A	1989	$23.95	$35
1989	5 In.	Baby Swan	N/A	1991	$12.95	$30
1989	5 In.	Lamb	N/A	1991	$14.95	$40
1989	5 In.	Sailor Duck	N/A	1991	$18.95	$55
1989	7 In.	Business Man Mouse	5,085	1989	$21.95	$45
1989	7 In.	Christmas Morning Kid Logo w/Pin	16,641	1990	$19.95	$70
1989	7 In.	Dragon Kid	4,651	1991	$29.95	$60
1989	7 In.	Dress up Boy	N/A	1990	$27.50	$35
1989	7 In.	Dress up Boy & Girl	N/A	1990	$55.00	$80
1989	7 In.	Duck Kid	4,020	1989	$25.95	$50
1989	7 In.	Ghost Kid	3,445	N/A	$29.95	$45
1989	7 In.	Knitting Mouse	5,115	1989	$19.95	$40
1989	7 In.	Polar Bear Club w/Plaque	3,000	1991	$37.50	$100
1989	7 In.	Pumpkin Kid	8,579	1992	$25.95	$55
1989	7 In.	Santa in Sleigh w/10 In. Reindeer	3,500	N/A	$52.95	$125
1989	7 In.	Science Center of N. H. Fishing Mouse	500	1989	$75.00	$125

Year Introduced	Size (Inches)	Doll	Edition Size	Year Retired	Issue Price	Value
1989	7 In.	Sweetheart Mouse	N/A	N/A	$16.95	$35
1989	7 In.	Tacky Tourist Mouse	5,116	1989	$19.95	$40
1989	10 In.	Abraham Lincoln w/Dome	2,500	1991	$120.00	$225-$275
1989	10 In.	Americana Couple w/Plaque	1,359	1990	$109.95	$150-$300
1989	10 In.	Barbecue Pig	2,471	1989	$27.95	$70
1989	10 In.	Bob Cratchett w/5 In. Tiny Tim (Artist Proof)**	3,832	1990	$99.95	$475
1989	10 In.	Bunnies (2 on Flexible Flyer Sled)	4,104	1989	$52.95	$115
1989	10 In.	Bunnies (3 on Revolving Maypole)	647	1989	$189.95	$300
1989	10 In.	Country Boy Bunny w/Basket	3,586	1989	$29.95	$85
1989	10 In.	Country Girl Bunny w/Flowers	3,789	1989	$29.95	$85-$125
1989	10 In.	Country Boy & Girl Goose	N/A	1989	$63.95	$135
1989	10 In.	Country Boy Pig	N/A	1989	$25.95	$65
1989	10 In.	Country Girl Pig	2,367	1989	$25.95	$65
1989	10 In.	E. P. Girl Bunny	N/A	1989	$31.95	$70
1989	10 In.	Merlin the Magician w/Brass Plaque	3,565	1990	$70.00	$115
1989	10 In.	Toy Soldier	2,734	N/A	$30.95	$50
1989	10 In.	Wiseman (2) w/Plaque	1,477	1990	$110.00	$240
1989	12 In.	Scarecrow (Blue Stone Washed)	6,070	1993	$31.95	$90
1989	12 In.	Trick or Treat Mouse	N/A	N/A	$39.95	$75
1989	18 In.	P. J. Kid Hanging Stocking	498	N/A	$39.95	$100-$125
1989	18 In.	Thorny the Ghost	N/A	1991	$51.95	$125
1989	18 In.	Witch	4,017	1992	$49.95	$100
1989	24 In.	Christmas Swan	N/A	1990	$62.95	$150
1989	24 In.	Spring Swan	N/A	1990	$59.95	$125
1989	30 In.	Toy Soldier	762	1989	$99.95	$300
1989	30 In.	Toy Soldier (Animated)	276	1989	$280.00	$625
1989	30 In.	Workshop Santa (Animated)	N/A	1989	N/A	$350

1982 – 12-inch Girl Skunk. It has a black body and wears a white dress. It holds a bouquet of pink and white flowers. $175.

1982 – 12-inch Boy Skunk. It has a black body and wears a green vest with white polka dots and a white collar. It holds a red Valentine box tied with green ribbon. $150.

1990s

1991 – These are 10-inch Bride and Groom Bears. The Bride Bear (left) wears a white wedding dress. $90. The Groom Bear (right) wears a black tuxedo and black hat. $85.

Year Introduced	Size (Inches)	Doll	Edition Size	Year Retired	Issue Price	Value
1990	5 In.	Christmas Dragon	7,420	1992	$21.59	$50
1990	5 In.	Valentine Dragon	4,135	1990	$25.95	$45
1990	7 In.	Angel on Sled w/Cloud	N/A	1991	$29.95	$65
1990	7 In.	Artist Mouse	7,285	1990	$23.95	$45
1990	7 In.	Clown Kid Logo w/Pin	20,049	1991	$19.95	$70
1990	7 In.	Friar Tuck Mouse (Artist Proof, signed)**	N/A	1990	$26.95	$300
1990	7 In.	Maui Mouse	7,220	1990	$23.95	$50
1990	7 In.	Robin Hood Mouse	6,838	1990	$26.50	$40
1990	7 In.	Sailor Mouse	6,838	1990	$23.95	$45
1990	7 In.	Thorndike Chicken w/Plaque	3,000	N/A	$37.50	$90
1990	10 In.	Annalee Collection Doll w/Dome	N/A	1991	$149.95	$225-$350
1990	10 In.	Betsy Ross w/Dome	2,500	1991	$119.50	$225-$275
1990	10 In.	Clown w/Stand (green)	2,750	1990	$27.95	$50
1990	10 In.	E. P. Boy & Girl Bunny	N/A	1990	$69.95	$130
1990	10 In.	Hobo Clown	4,898	1991	$23.95	$60
1990	10 In.	Jacob Marley w/Plaque	516	1992	$89.95	$175
1990	10 In.	N. H. Musical Conductor	N/A	1991	$110.00	$295-$450
1990	10 In.	Santa Pig	N/A	1991	$31.95	$65
1990	10 In.	Spirit of 76 w/Dome	556	1991	$174.95	$295-$450
1990	10 In.	Strawberry Girl Bunny	582	1990	$34.95	$100
1990	10 In.	Wiseman w/Camel w/Plaque**	387	1991	$110.00	$250-$295
1990	10 In.	Wiseman w/Camel (Artist Proof)**	N/A	1991	$110.00	$600
1990	12 In.	Easter Duck w/Watering Can	2,891	1991	$49.50	$80
1990	12 In.	P. J. Kid (Red Hair)	2,307	N/A	$29.95	$70
1990	12 In.	Santa Duck	506	1991	$49.95	$95-$150
1990	15 In.	Christmas Dragon	3,703	1990	$49.95	$100
1990	18 In.	Angel w/Instrument	398	1991	$55.95	$110-$125
1990	18 In.	Bunny Kid w/Slipper	4,530	1992	$49.95	$100
1990	18 In.	Choir Girl	N/A	1991	$57.95	$90
1990	18 In.	Christmas Morning Kid w/Train	N/A	1990	$65.59	$125
1990	18 In.	Day After Christmas Santa (Proto Type)** 1		1991	N/A	$250
1990	18 In.	Dragon Kid	1,257	1990	$69.95	$160
1990	18 In.	E. P. Boy Bunny	N/A	1990	$69.95	$95
1990	18 In.	Girl on Sled	N/A	1990	$55.95	$125
1990	18 In.	Naughty Kid	1,454	1991	$69.95	$140
1990	18 In.	Pumpkin Kid (One of a Kind)**	1	1991	$69.95	$275
1990	18 In.	Strawberry Girl Bunny	2,365	1990	$59.95	$110
1990	18 In.	Trick or Treat Bunny Kid	N/A	1991	$49.95	$150
1990	20 In.	Spring Elf (Pink)	1,990	1990	$34.95	$100-$125
1990	20 In.	Spring Elf (Yellow)	N/A	1990	$34.95	$100-$125
1990	30 In.	Angel	N/A	1990	$75.95	$150
1990	30 In.	Clown w/Stand	530	1990	$99.50	$150
1990	30 In.	Strawberry Bunny (Girl)	582	N/A	$135.95	$225
1991	3 In.	Water Baby in Pond Lilly	3,720	1991	$14.95	$40
1991	5 In.	Angel	9,844	N/A	$22.95	$40
1991	5 In.	Baby Swan	3,168	N/A	$13.95	$35
1991	5 In.	Christmas Dragon	4,125	N/A	$23.95	$50
1991	5 In.	Duck on Flexible Flyer Sled	3,822	N/A	$25.95	$45
1991	5 In.	Easter Parade Boy Duck	4,261	1991	$22.00	$35

1990 – 7-inch Angel on Sled with Cloud. The doll has a gold halo and white felt wings. It wears a blue scarf and rides a flexible flyer sled. $65.

1990 – 7-inch Robin Hood Mouse wearing a green hat, green shirt and brown belt. It comes with a bow and two arrows. $40.

1990 – 7-inch Friar Tuck Mouse dressed in brown hat and brown robe with white rope belt. It holds a walking stick. $45 ($300 for a signed artist proof).

** Signed by Annalee

1990 – 10-inch Jacob Marley with white hair. It wears a black suit, gray vest and black tie. It is wrapped in chains and holds a ledger book. $175.

1990 – 10-inch Annalee Collector Doll with glass dome and wooden base (signed Artist Proof). The edition was numbered. Annalee wears a pink outfit and black boots, and holds a snowman and a baby girl with two other babies holding her legs. $295.

Year Introduced	Size (Inches)	Doll	Edition Size	Year Retired	Issue Price	Value
1991	5 In.	Easter Parade Girl Duck	5,105	1991	$24.00	$35
1991	5 In.	Elf (Workshop)	16,359	N/A	$13.45	$25
1991	5 In.	Fawn (Spotted)	13,027	1991	$14.45	$25
1991	5 In.	Fluffy Yellow Chick	6,979	1992	$15.95	$45
1991	5 In.	Leprechaun	6,384	N/A	$15.95	$30
1991	5 In.	Sailor Duck	2,241	N/A	$21.95	$40
1991	5 In.	Spring Lamb	6,709	1992	$16.95	$35
1991	5 In.	Trim A Tree Elf	10,108	N/A	$12.95	$20
1991	5 In.	Winter Duck in Inner Tube	2,992	N/A	$23.95	$55
1991	7 In.	Angel on Sled w/Cloud	2,313	N/A	$29.95	$65
1991	7 In.	Angel w/Musical Instrument	5,879	N/A	$19.95	$30
1991	7 In.	Artist Bunny	N/A	1995	$20.95	$40
1991	7 In.	Baker Mouse	6,895	1991	$25.95	$45
1991	7 In.	Ben Franklin Mouse	5,029	1991	$29.95	$50
1991	7 In.	Bunny Kid	3,827	N/A	$23.45	$50
1991	7 In.	Caroler Boy	510	N/A	$22.95	$30
1991	7 In.	Caroler Boy Mouse w/Music	7,281	N/A	$22.95	$45
1991	7 In.	Caroler Girl	5,134	N/A	$22.95	$30
1991	7 In.	Christmas Gnome	15,503	1993	$17.95	$45
1991	7 In.	Country Boy Bunny	N/A	1991	$28.95	$30
1991	7 In.	Desert Storm Mouse Head Pin	N/A	1991	$7.95	$30
1991	7 In.	Desert Storm Nurse Mouse Pin	N/A	1991	$7.95	$50
1991	7 In.	Dragon Kid	1,116	N/A	$31.95	$50
1991	7 In.	Drummer Boy	7,031	N/A	$22.45	$50
1991	7 In.	Earth Day Mouse	5,863	N/A	$29.95	$50
1991	7 In.	Easter Parade Boy	7,043	N/A	$27.45	$40
1991	7 In.	Easter Parade Girl	9,120	N/A	$18.95	$40
1991	7 In.	Flying Angel w/Mistletoe	6,003	N/A	$18.95	$30
1991	7 In.	Fun In the Sun w/Pin (tag signed by Annalee)	300	1991	$80.00	$295-$335
1991	7 In.	Ghost Kid w/Pumpkin	1,982	N/A	$24.45	$55
1991	7 In.	Gnome w/Mushroom	5,007	N/A	$29.95	$60
1991	7 In.	Indian Boy	3,371	N/A	$29.95	$50
1991	7 In.	Indian Girl	2,777	1991	$29.95	$50
1991	7 In.	Mouse in Box	5,526	N/A	$19.95	$40
1991	7 In.	Mouse in Santa's Hat	9,742	N/A	$17.95	$25
1991	7 In.	Mouse w/Candy Cane	5,206	N/A	$17.95	$40
1991	7 In.	Mouse w/Christmas Stocking	6,543	N/A	$17.95	$35
1991	7 In.	Mouse w/Mail Bag	14,546	1993	$25.95	$40
1991	7 In.	Mouse w/Presents	8,075	N/A	$17.95	$40
1991	7 In.	Mouse w/Snowball	6,805	N/A	$17.95	$35
1991	7 In.	Mouse w/Tennis Racquet	5,674	N/A	$21.95	$45
1991	7 In.	Mrs. Santa Hanging Merry	11,769	1993	$27.95	$40
1991	7 In.	Pilgrim Kids w/Basket	2,672	N/A	$53.95	$85
1991	7 In.	Pilgrim Mice Set w/Basket	2,721	N/A	$42.45	$75
1991	7 In.	Pumpkin Kid	3,517	N/A	$27.45	$50
1991	7 In.	Reading Kid w/Pin	26,516	1992	$19.95	$80
1991	7 In.	Red Cross Nurse Mouse	8,305	N/A	$29.95	$45
1991	7 In.	Ritz Snowman	10,309	N/A	$27.95	$45
1991	7 In.	Santa Bringing Home Christmas Tree	8,604	1993	$27.95	$60

Year Introduced	Size (Inches)	Doll	Edition Size	Year Retired	Issue Price	Value
1991	7 In.	Santa Humbug Merry Christmas Sign	11,769	1993	$27.95	$40
1991	7 In.	Santa in Tub w/Rubber Ducky	5,373	N/A	$33.95	$55
1991	7 In.	Santa w/Gift List & Toy Bag	8,886	N/A	$22.45	$30
1991	7 In.	Santa w/Mailbag & Letters	12,156	1993	$27.95	$50
1991	7 In.	Mrs. Santa w/Presents	7,863	N/A	$26.45	$35
1991	7 In.	Santa w/Sleigh	3,407	N/A	$26.45	$50
1991	7 In.	Secretary Mouse	6,394	1991	$29.95	$60
1991	7 In.	Sheriff Mouse w/Plaque	1,191	1991	$49.95	$95
1991	7 In.	Skeleton Costume Kid	2,596	N/A	$24.45	$50
1991	7 In.	Sledding Mouse	5,950	1991	$20.95	$40
1991	7 In.	Snowman w/Pipe	7,401	N/A	$23.95	$45
1991	7 In.	Sweetheart Boy Mouse	7,865	1991	$19.95	$35
1991	7 In.	Sweetheart Girl Mouse	7,865	1991	$19.95	$30
1991	7 In.	Trick or Treat Bunny Kid	2,187	1991	$25.95	$50
1991	7 In.	Mr. & Mrs. Tuckered Mouse	13,266	1993	$19.95	$65
1991	7 In.	Two in a Tent Mice	N/A	N/A	$34.95	$95
1991	7 In.	Velour Mrs. Santa w/Coat	5,808	N/A	$27.45	$30
1991	7 In.	Velour Santa w/Coat & Pipe	N/A	N/A	$27.45	$30
1991	7 In.	Video Mouse	4,978	N/A	$26.00	$45
1991	7 In.	Waiter Mouse	4,573	1991	$29.95	$45
1991	7 In.	Witch Kid	3,311	1991	$27.45	$50
1991	7 In.	Workshop Mouse	12,536	N/A	$21.95	$40
1991	7 In.	Workshop Santa	3,872	N/A	$26.95	$30
1991	8 In.	Boy Turkey	2,586	N/A	$35.00	$60
1991	8 In.	Boy Turkey w/7 In. Indian Girl	1,658	N/A	$58.00	$85
1991	10 In.	Annalee Collector Doll w/Dome	588	N/A	$149.95	$225
1991	10 In.	Aviator Frog	2,110	1991	$19.95	$60
1991	10 In.	Bat	N/A	1992	$31.95	$80
1991	10 In.	Bear in Nightshirt w/Candle	2,774	N/A	$32.95	$60
1991	10 In.	Bear in Velour Santa Suit	3,711	N/A	$32.95	$60
1991	10 In.	Bear w/Snowball w/Knit Hat	3,121	N/A	$29.95	$60
1991	10 In.	Black Cat	6,267	1992	$21.95	$80
1991	10 In.	Bob Cratchett & 5 In. Tiny Tim	639	N/A	$99.95	$160
1991	10 In.	Bride Bear	2,977	1991	$40.00	$90
1991	10 In.	Bride & Groom Bear	N/A	1991	$79.50	$165
1991	10 In.	Christmas Elf	16,567	N/A	$15.95	$25
1991	10 In.	Christopher Columbus w/Dome	1,132	N/A	$119.50	$275
1991	10 In.	N. H. Musical Conductor	383	1991	$129.50	$295-$450
1991	10 In.	Country Boy Bunny w/Wheelbarrow	1,844	1991	$42.95	$75
1991	10 In.	Country Girl Bunny w/Flowers	2,044	1991	$34.95	$75
1991	10 In.	Doe	6,541	N/A	$20.95	$35
1991	10 In.	Easter Parade Boy Bunny	4,195	N/A	$38.95	$75
1991	10 In.	Easter Parade Girl Bunny	5,101	N/A	$38.95	$75
1991	10 In.	Gingerbread Boy	10,453	1994	$22.45	$45
1991	10 In.	Girl w/Basket	3,592	1991	$37.95	$70
1991	10 In.	Groom Bear	2,745	1991	$39.95	$85
1991	10 In.	Hobo Clown	2,368	N/A	$25.45	$60
1991	10 In.	Huskie w/5 In. Puppy in Dog Sled	2,860	1991	$54.95	$100
1991	10 In.	Indian Man	2,719	N/A	$32.95	$65
1991	10 In.	Indian Woman	2,779	1991	$32.95	$65

1990 – 10-inch Hobo Clown wearing polka-dotted orange-and-white pants, green shirt, red tie and black hat with daisy. It holds a balloon. $60.

1990 – 10-inch Wise Man and Camel with brass plaque. The Wise Man has a black beard and wears a purple and red robe with gold trim. It holds onto a camel and its riding strap. $250-$295 (signed by Annalee).

1990 – 30-inch Clown wearing yellow suit, hat and shoes. It is on a gray wooden stand. $150.

Year Introduced	Size (Inches)	Doll	Edition Size	Year Retired	Issue Price	Value
1991	10 In.	Kitten w/Knit Mittens	4,124	N/A	$33.95	$55
1991	10 In.	Kitten on Sled	3,810	N/A	$35.95	$65
1991	10 In.	Large Pumpkin	1,872	N/A	$48.95	$80
1991	10 In.	Man & Woman Skaters	N/A	1992	$91.90	$165
1991	10 In.	Martha Cratchett w/Plaque	2,136	1992	$59.95	$150
1991	10 In.	Nativity Angel w/ Dome	2,112	1991	$59.95	$110
1991	10 In.	Nativity Set	658	N/A	$149.95	$275
1991	10 In.	Pilgrim Man w/Basket	2,374	N/A	$44.95	$75
1991	10 In.	Pilgrim Woman w/Turkey	2,502	1992	$44.95	$75
1991	10 In.	Reindeer w/Cap & Bell	10,300	N/A	$22.45	$25
1991	10 In.	Santa Feeding Reindeer	2,618	N/A	$79.95	$125
1991	10 In.	Santa Pig	2,685	N/A	$31.95	$65
1991	10 In.	Santa on Rocking Horse	2,398	N/A	$49.95	$100
1991	10 In.	Santa Playing w/Train	1,525	N/A	$49.95	$100
1991	10 In.	Santa w/Reindeer Golfing	2,462	N/A	$79.95	$130
1991	10 In.	Scrooge	592	N/A	$89.95	$150
1991	10 In.	Shepherd Boy & Lamb**	591	N/A	$89.95	$175-$295
1991	10 In.	Skating Bunny	6,027	1992	$43.95	$80
1991	10 In.	Skating Man	4,881	1992	$46.00	$85
1991	10 In.	Snowy Owl	3,163	N/A	$25.95	$60
1991	10 In.	Spider	N/A	1992	$38.95	$65
1991	10 In.	Spring Elf	4,060	N/A	$15.95	$45
1991	10 In.	Summer Santa	1,926	1991	$59.95	$95
1991	10 In.	The Spirit of 76 w/Dome	1,080	N/A	$175.00	$295-$450
1991	10 In.	Tinsel Elf	17,070	N/A	$20.45	$45
1991	10 In.	Two Wise Men w/Plaque	476	N/A	$109.95	$240
1991	10 In.	Victory Ski Doll w/ Plaque	1,192	N/A	$49.50	$100
1991	10 In.	Wise Man w/Camel w/Plaque**	476	N/A	$109.95	$200-$250

1990 – 18-inch Angel with Instrument holding onto a brass horn. The angel has white felt wings, gold halo. $110.

1990 – 18-inch Bunny Kid with Bunny Slippers wearing white outfit and pink and white bunny slippers. The doll has pink ears. $100.

Year Introduced	Size (Inches)	Doll	Edition Size	Year Retired	Issue Price	Value
1991	10 In.	Woman Skater	4,975	N/A	$45.95	$85
1991	12 In.	Basket Couple	2,028	N/A	$96.95	$100
1991	12 In.	Bat	3,113	1992	$29.95	$75
1991	12 In.	Christmas Swan	674	1991	$63.95	$110
1991	12 In.	Drummer Boy	3,298	N/A	$39.95	$55
1991	12 In.	Easter Duck w/Watering Can	1,407	N/A	$49.95	$95
1991	12 In.	Pilgrim Boy Mouse	1,980	1991	$42.95	$95-$100
1991	12 In.	Pilgrim Girl Mouse	1,978	1991	$42.95	$95-$100
1991	12 In.	P. J. Kid (Blonde Hair)	2,726	1992	$29.95	$60
1991	12 In.	P. J. Kid (Brown Hair)	2,307	1992	$29.95	$60
1991	12 In.	P. J. Kid (Red Hair)	n/a	1991	$29.95	$70
1991	12 In.	Santa Duck	1,187	N/A	$53.45	$95
1991	12 In.	Santa w/Potbellied Stove	5,887	N/A	$59.45	$85
1991	12 In.	Santa's Helper Painting Boat	5,274	1991	$35.95	$75
1991	12 In.	Santa's Postman w/Cardholder Mailbag	6,980	1993	$35.95	$75
1991	12 In.	Scarecrow	2,330	N/A	$40.95	$75
1991	12 In.	Spider	5,194	1992	$32.95	$95
1991	12 In.	Spring Swan	615	N/A	$49.95	$125
1991	12 In.	Tree Top Angel	2,589	1991	$42.45	$65
1991	12 In.	Tuckered Couple	2,574	1994	$89.95	$125
1991	12 In.	Turkey	1,132	N/A	$58.00	$110
1991	12 In.	Velour Mrs. Santa	3,677	N/A	$49.95	$60
1991	12 In.	Velour Santa w/Toy Bag	3,517	N/A	$49.95	$75
1991	14 In.	Pumpkin Solid	1,872	N/A	$49.00	$125
1991	15 In.	Hobo Clown	1,295	1991	$47.50	$125
1991	18 In.	Reindeer w/Christmas Saddlebags	4,053	N/A	$53.00	$75-$95
1991	18 In.	Angel w/Instrument	1,009	N/A	$55.45	$125

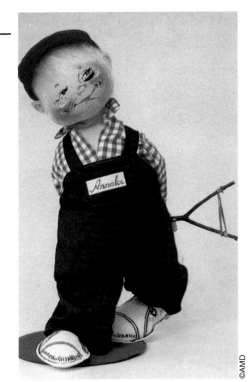

1990 – 18-inch Naughty Kid with blonde hair. It wears a red checkered shirt, blue denim overalls, red hat and white shoes. The doll holds a sling shot. $140.

1990 – 20-inch Spring Elf with blonde hair. The doll wears a pink suit outfit. $100.

1991 – 7-inch Reading Logo Kid with blonde hair. The doll wears a red-and-white outfit and black shoes. It sits on an ABC block reading a book. $80.

1991 – 7-inch Secretary Mouse with white hair and pink ears. It wears a green-and-white plaid dress and glasses. The doll stands on a brown platform getting ready to smash its computer with a hammer. $60.

1991 – 7-inch Sheriff Mouse with plaque. It wears a tan uniform and tan hat, and comes with a belt holster, gun and sheriff's badge. $95.

1991 – 7-inch Video Mouse wearing a green hat, green jacket and black shoes. The doll has a camera around its neck and carries a video camera. $45.

Year Introduced	Size (Inches)	Doll	Edition Size	Year Retired	Issue Price	Value
1991	18 In.	Bunny Kid w/Bunny Slipper	2,859	N/A	$49.95	$100
1991	18 In.	Chef Santa	4,511	N/A	$46.95	$125-$150
1991	18 In.	Choir Boy	3,120	N/A	$57.95	$125
1991	18 In.	Choir Girl	2,188	N/A	$57.95	$100
1991	18 In.	Day After Christmas Santa	2,263	N/A	$79.45	$140
1991	18 In.	Easter Parade Boy Bunny	2,056	N/A	$62.95	$90
1991	18 In.	Easter Parade Girl Bunny	2,254	N/A	$62.95	$90
1991	18 In.	Gingerbread Boy	3,966	1992	$50.95	$135
1991	18 In.	Mrs. Santa w/Presents	5,497	N/A	$49.95	$85
1991	18 In.	Mrs. Santa w/Tray	5,143	N/A	$49.95	$100
1991	18 In.	Naughty Kid	547	N/A	$74.95	$125
1991	18 In.	P. J. Kid	1,307	1991	$39.95	$85
1991	18 In.	P. J. Kid Hanging Stocking	1,396	1991	$46.95	$105
1991	18 In.	Pumpkin Kid	1,317	N/A	$74.45	$150
1991	18 In.	Reindeer w/Saddlebags	4,053	N/A	$52.95	$85
1991	18 In.	Santa w/Cardholder Mailbag	8,056	1992	$59.95	$90
1991	18 In.	Santa w/Gift List	6,334	N/A	$43.95	$55
1991	18 In.	Santa w/Stocking	4,466	N/A	$47.95	$75
1991	18 In.	Snowman w/Broom	4,218	N/A	$43.45	$75
1991	18 In.	Snowy Owl	965	N/A	$65.95	$150
1991	18 In.	Thorny the Ghost	1,270	N/A	$51.95	$125
1991	18 In.	Trick or Treat Bunny Kid	625	N/A	$49.95	$125
1991	18 In.	Witch	2,033	N/A	$63.95	$100
1991	22 In.	Christmas Stocking	4,993	N/A	$18.45	$45
1991	22 In.	Red Christmas Elf	3,679	N/A	$34.95	$50
1991	30 In.	Mrs. & Mrs. Tuckered w/2 P. J. Kids	644	N/A	$291.45	$350
1991	30 In.	Mrs. Santa w/Cardholder	1,483	N/A	$119.95	$140
1991	30 In.	Santa w/Lighted Tree	509	N/A	$189.95	$220
1991	30 In.	Velour Mrs. Santa w/Muff	755	N/A	$160.45	$200
1991	30 In.	Velour Santa w/Pipe & Bag	1,221	N/A	$160.45	$160-$195
1991	36 In.	Reindeer (Animated)	134	N/A	$339.95	$450
1991	36 In.	Reindeer w/Cardholder	879	N/A	$148.45	$225-$295
1992	3 In.	Sun Head Floral	5,419	N/A	$6.00	$15
1992	3 In.	Sun Magnet	7,133	N/A	$6.00	$10
1992	3 In.	Sun Pin	6,395	N/A	$6.00	$10
1992	5 In.	Angel on Cloud	7,967	1992	$22.95	$30
1992	5 In.	Christmas Dragon	3,132	1992	$23.95	$50
1992	5 In.	Christmas Lamb (White)	10,104	1996	$17.95	$35
1992	5 In.	Duck on Flexible Flyer	3,124	1992	$25.95	$45
1992	5 In.	Easter Parade Boy Duck	3,370	N/A	$23.95	$25
1992	5 In.	Easter Parade Girl Duck	4,468	N/A	$23.95	$45
1992	5 In.	Elf (Workshop)	13,825	1992	$13.45	$25
1992	5 In.	Equestrian Kid on 10 In. Horse (Plaque)	1,063	1992	$74.95	$105
1992	5 In.	Fawn	10,939	N/A	$14.45	$25
1992	5 In.	Fluffy Yellow Chick	4,342	1992	$17.95	$45
1992	5 In.	Leprechaun	4,705	1992	$15.95	$25
1992	5 In.	Raincoat Duck	5,397	1994	$26.95	$50
1992	5 In.	Spring Lamb	5,053	N/A	$17.95	$35
1992	5 In.	Trim A Tree Elf	11,985	N/A	$12.95	$20
1992	7 In.	Angel on Moon (White)	2,885	1992	$39.95	$100

a Year Introduced	Size (Inches)	Doll	Edition Size	Year Retired	Issue Price	Value
1992	7 In.	Angel w/Musical Instrument	6,347	N/A	$19.95	$30
1992	7 In.	Artist Bunny w/Brush	5,346	1992	$20.95	$40
1992	7 In.	Baby New Year	6,254	1993	$26.95	$55
1992	7 In.	Back to School Kid w/Pin	17,524	1993	$25.00	$55
1992	7 In.	Ballerina Kid	4,553	1993	$27.95	$55
1992	7 In.	Ballerina Kid on Music Box	2,718	N/A	$41.95	$95
1992	7 In.	Beach Kid w/Boat	3,817	1992	$29.95	$50
1992	7 In.	Birthday Girl Mouse	9,592	N/A	$23.95	$40
1992	7 In.	Bride & Groom Bunny	5,929	1993	$45.95	$100 set
1992	7 In.	Bunny in Slipper (Yellow)	6,338	1993	$19.95	$45
1992	7 In.	Caroler Boy	4,606	1992	$22.95	$35
1992	7 In.	Caroler Girl	4,913	1992	$22.95	$35
1992	7 In.	Caroler Mouse w/Hat & Tree	18,789	1995	$19.95	$35
1992	7 In.	Caroling Mouse	N/A	N/A	N/A	$35
1992	7 In.	Champagne Mouse in Glass (New Years)	9,553	1994	$25.95	$55
1992	7 In.	Chef Santa	11,297	1996	$28.95	$50
1992	7 In.	Christmas Gnome	9,102	N/A	$18.95	$45
1992	7 In.	Country Boy Bunny	3,993	N/A	$20.45	$35
1992	7 In.	Country Girl Bunny	3,937	1992	$20.45	$30
1992	7 In.	Desert Storm Mouse	3,114	1992	$29.95	$50
1992	7 In.	Devil Kid	6,076	1993	$23.95	$55
1992	7 In.	Dracula Kid	5,637	1994	$25.95	$50
1992	7 In.	Drummer Boy	7,297	1992	$22.45	$40
1992	7 In.	Easter Parade (Boy) Bunny	6,668	N/A	$20.95	$35
1992	7 In.	Easter Parade (Girl) Bunny	9,314	N/A	$20.95	$35
1992	7 In.	Fishing Mouse	6,145	N/A	$31.95	$55
1992	7 In.	Flying Angel w/Mistletoe	6,457	N/A	$18.95	$30
1992	7 In.	Gnome w/Mushroom	1,691	N/A	$35.95	$60
1992	7 In.	Golfer Mouse	7,435	N/A	$26.95	$55
1992	7 In.	Greenthumb Mouse	5,995	1992	$25.95	$45
1992	7 In.	Groom Bunny	5,578	N/A	$22.95	$50
1992	7 In.	Housewife Mouse (Vacuum)	N/A	1992	$25.95	$65
1992	7 In.	Indian Boy	2,315	1992	$29.95	$50
1992	7 In.	Indian Girl	2,297	1992	$29.95	$50
1992	7 In.	Kid w/Kite	3,850	N/A	$29.95	$50
1992	7 In.	Ladybug Kid	4,970	1993	$29.95	$45
1992	7 In.	Mouse in Box	4,994	1992	$19.95	$40
1992	7 In.	Mouse in Cornucopia	7,833	N/A	$22.95	$45
1992	7 In.	Mouse in Santa's Hat	10,941	N/A	$17.95	$25
1992	7 In.	Mouse on Cheese	14,923	1993	$25.95	$45
1992	7 In.	Mouse w/Mailbag & Letters	8,000	1992	$25.95	$45
1992	7 In.	Mouse w/North Pole	10,089	N/A	$21.95	$45
1992	7 In.	Mouse w/Presents	N/A	1992	$17.95	$40
1992	7 In.	Mouse w/Snowball	7,095	1992	$17.95	$35
1992	7 In.	Mouse w/Tennis Racquet Snowshoes	4,110	1992	$21.95	$45
1992	7 In.	Mr. Tuckered Mouse	7,533	1992	$19.95	$35
1992	7 In.	Mrs. Tuckered Mouse	8,321	1992	$19.95	$35
1992	7 In.	Mrs. Santa Hanging Merry Christmas	6,411	N/A	$27.95	$40

1991 – 7-inch Waiter Mouse wearing a white shirt and black bow tie. It holds a platter in its right arm with a towel in its left. $45.

1991 – 10-inch Girl with Basket with blonde hair. It wears a green hat and cape, brown shoes and red gloves. It carries a basket filled with holly. $70.

1991 – 10-inch Skating Bunny with pink ears. The doll wears a pink outfit trimmed in white and white skates. $80.

Year Introduced	Size (Inches)	Doll	Edition Size	Year Retired	Issue Price	Value
1992	7 In.	Mrs. Santa w/Poinsettia	11,484	N/A	$29.95	$35
1992	7 In.	Mrs. Santa w/Presents	7,124	N/A	$27.95	$35
1992	7 In.	Nick w/Pin** (Disney Exclusive)	300	1992	$94.95	$325
1992	7 In.	Pilgrim Kid w/Basket	2,303	1992	$53.95	$85
1992	7 In.	Pilgrim Mice Set w/Basket	2,364	N/A	$42.95	$75
1992	7 In.	Pirate Kid	5,412	1994	$23.95	$50
1992	7 In.	Pumpkin Kid	3,619	1992	$27.45	$50
1992	7 In.	Red Cross Nurse Mouse	N/A	N/A	$29.95	$30
1992	7 In.	Ritz Snowman	6,037	1992	$26.95	$45
1992	7 In.	Santa Bringing Home Christmas Tree	5,921	N/A	$27.95	$45
1992	7 In.	Mrs. Santa Cardholder	9,831	N/A	$25.95	$50
1992	7 In.	Santa in Chimney	8,119	N/A	$33.95	$45
1992	7 In.	Santa on Moon	4,157	1992	$46.95	$95
1992	7 In.	Santa w/Gift List & Toy Bag	7,815	1992	$23.95	$25
1992	7 In.	Santa w/Mailbag & Letters	7,493	N/A	$27.95	$50
1992	7 In.	Santa & Mrs. Santa w/Candle Holder	9,595	1993	$51.95	$100
1992	7 In.	Santa w/Presents	6,594	N/A	$23.95	$30
1992	7 In.	Santa Skunk	6,753	1993	$27.95	$50
1992	7 In.	Scarecrow Kid	4,595	1993	$27.95	$50
1992	7 In.	Schoolgirl Kid w/Pin	17,524	1993	$24.95	$60
1992	7 In.	Sheriff Mouse w/Plaque	283	N/A	$49.95	$100
1992	7 In.	Skateboard Kid	3,894	1992	$29.95	$45
1992	7 In.	Sledding Mouse	6,247	1992	$20.95	$40

1991 – 12-inch Santa's Helper Painting Boat. The doll is dressed in a light green jacket, dark green hat and shirt and red pants. It holds the boat in one hand and a paint brush in the other. $75.

1991 – 7-inch Trick or Treat Bunny Kid and 7-inch Witch Kid. The Bunny Kid (left) wears a white suit with long orange bunny ears and orange bow tie. The doll carries a trick-or-treat bag. $50. The Witch Kid wears a black coat, hat and mask and orange sneakers. The doll holds a broom in one hand and a trick-or-treat bag in the other. $50.

Year Introduced	Size (Inches)	Doll	Edition Size	Year Retired	Issue Price	Value
1992	7 In.	Snowman w/Pipe	7,779	1992	$23.95	$45
1992	7 In.	Spring Girl Chicken w/Boa	2,753	1993	$34.95	$60
1992	7 In.	Spring Skunk	1,590	1993	$22.95	$45
1992	7 In.	Sweetheart Boy Mouse	5,723	N/A	$18.95	$30
1992	7 In.	Sweetheart Girl Mouse	6,522	N/A	$18.95	$30
1992	7 In.	Two in a Tent Mice	2,910	N/A	$34.95	$95
1992	7 In.	Witch Kid	3,592	1992	$27.95	$55
1992	7 In.	Workshop Mouse	6,618	1992	$21.95	$40
1992	10 In.	Baseball Player	5,760	N/A	$29.95	$75
1992	10 In.	Baseball Pitcher	1,283	N/A	$36.00	$75
1992	10 In.	Bear in Nightshirt	3,434	N/A	$33.95	$60
1992	10 In.	Bear in Velour Santa Suit	3,938	1992	$32.95	$60
1992	10 In.	Bear w/Snowball Knit Hat	3,826	1992	$29.95	$60
1992	10 In.	Black Cat	4,101	1992	$25.95	$75
1992	10 In.	Christmas Elf	18,130	N/A	$15.95	$25
1992	10 In.	Christmas Eve Bob Cratchett w/Plaque	1,681	1992	$69.95	$200
1992	10 In.	Christmas Eve Scrooge w/Plaque	1,722	1992	$59.95	$195
1992	10 In.	Country Boy Bunny w/Butterfly	2,395	N/A	$34.95	$55
1992	10 In.	Country Girl Bunny w/Flowers	2,577	1992	$34.95	$55
1992	10 In.	Doe	2,096	1992	$20.95	$35
1992	10 In.	Easter Parade Boy Bunny	3,902	1992	$38.95	$65
1992	10 In.	Easter Parade Girl Bunny	4,832	1992	$38.95	$65
1992	10 In.	Father Time	1,796	1993	$54.95	$100
1992	10 In.	Fishing Santa and Mrs in Boat w/Plaque	1,582	1992	$99.95	$165-$200
1992	10 In.	Frog in Boat	3,231	1993	$31.95	$65
1992	10 In.	Gingerbread Boy	7,361	1992	$22.45	$45
1992	10 In.	Indian Man	1,834	1992	$34.45	$60
1992	10 In.	Indian Woman	1,816	1992	$32.95	$60
1992	10 In.	Jacob Marley w/Plaque	672	1992	$89.95	$175
1992	10 In.	Kitten w/Knit Mittens	4,004	1992	$33.95	$55
1992	10 In.	Leprechaun w/Pot O' Gold	N/A	1992	$20.95	$60
1992	10 In.	Man & Woman Skater	2,754	1992	$45.95	$85
1992	10 In.	Martha Cratchett w/Plum Pudding	784	1992	$59.95	$150
1992	10 In.	Mrs. Bear in Nightshirt w/Candle	4,661	1993	$38.95	$75
1992	10 In.	Pilgrim Man w/Basket	1,803	1992	$44.95	$75
1992	10 In.	Pilgrim Woman w/Turkey	1,904	1992	$44.95	$75
1992	10 In.	Reindeer w/Cap & Bell	2,096	1992	$22.95	$25
1992	10 In.	Santa at Workbench	2,209	1992	$69.95	$125
1992	10 In.	Saving Santa	1,605	1992	$59.95	$95
1992	10 In.	Skating Bunny	4,005	1992	$44.00	$80
1992	10 In.	Snow Queen	4,390	N/A	$38.95	$80
1992	10 In.	Snowy Owl	2,634	N/A	$25.95	$60
1992	10 In.	Spider**	N/A	NA	N/A	$250
1992	10 In.	Spider	N/A	N/A	N/A	$75
1992	10 In.	Tennis Santa	2,115	1992	$49.95	$95
1992	10 In.	Tinsel the Elf	9,967	1992	$20.45	$45
1992	10 In.	Uncle Sam Folk Hero	1,034	1993	$87.50	$275-$300
1992	10 In.	Woman Skater	2,754	1992	$46	$85
1992	12 In.	Basket Couple	N/A	N/A	$60	$75

1991 – 18-inch Gingerbread Boy wearing a brown jacket trimmed in white. $135.

1991 – 18-inch P.J. Kids. The P.J. Kid (right) has auburn hair and wears a white outfit with holly print. $85. The P.J. Kid Hanging Stocking (left) has auburn hair and wears a white outfit with holly print. It holds a red, fur-trimmed stocking. $105.

1992 – 5-inch Christmas Dragon with dark green body and light green face. The doll wears a white and red Santa hat and holds a Christmas gift. $50.

1992 – 5-inch Duck on Flexible Flyer wearing a green-and-white striped scarf. $45.

1992 – Two 5-inch Fluffy Yellow Chicks with yellow face, white hair, yellow feet and white body. $45.

Year Introduced	Size (Inches)	Doll	Edition Size	Year Retired	Issue Price	Value
1992	12 In.	Bat	2,107	1992	$31.95	$75
1992	12 In.	Chef Santa	3,353	1992	$44.95	$75
1992	12 In.	Drummer Boy	3,316	1992	$39.95	$55
1992	12 In.	Mrs. Santa w/Poinsettia	3,463	1992	$49.95	$75
1992	12 In.	Pilgrim Boy Mouse	1,449	1992	$42.95	$85
1992	12 In.	Pilgrim Girl Mouse	1,474	1992	$42.95	$85
1992	12 In.	P. J. Boy	7,526	1993	$29.95	$70
1992	12 In.	P. J. Girl	7,903	1993	$29.95	$70
1992	12 In.	Santa w/Potbellied Stove	1,818	1992	$61.95	$85
1992	12 In.	Santa's Helper Painting Boat	2,737	1992	$38.95	$65
1992	12 In.	Santa's Postman w/Cardholder Mailbag	3,650	N/A	$39.95	$75
1992	12 In.	Scarecrow	1,873	N/A	$41.95	$75
1992	12 In.	Snowman	5,457	1993	$41.95	$75
1992	12 In.	Spider	3,461	1992	$38.95	$95
1992	12 In.	North Pole w/Snow	2,511	N/A	$8.95	$20
1992	12 In.	Tuckered Couple	1,827	1992	$89.95	$125
1992	12 In.	Velour Mrs. Santa	2,160	1992	$49.95	$50
1992	12 In.	Velour Santa w/Toy Bag	2,284	N/A	$49.95	$50
1992	14 In.	Pumpkin (Solid)	2,469	N/A	$48.50	$125
1992	14 In.	Uncle Sam Folk Hero	1,034	N/A	$87.50	$275-$300
1992	17 In.	Reindeer w/Christmas Saddlebags	3,441	N/A	$53.00	$85
1992	18 In.	Bunny Kid w/Bunny Slipper	2,117	1992	$49.95	$95
1992	18 In.	Chef Santa (Pie)	5,314	N/A	$47.95	$105
1992	18 In.	Country Boy Bunny	N/A	N/A	$54.95	$90
1992	18 In.	Easter Parade Boy Bunny	1,695	N/A	$65.95	$90
1992	18 In.	Easter Parade Girl Bunny	1,918	N/A	$65.95	$85
1992	18 In.	Gingerbread Boy (Green Jacket)	2,969	1992	$50.95	$135
1992	18 In.	Girl Bunny w/Flowers	1,501	N/A	$54.95	$95
1992	18 In.	Mrs. Santa w/Poinsettia	6,790	N/A	$53.95	$70
1992	18 In.	Mrs. Santa w/Presents	4,314	1992	$52.95	$85
1992	18 In.	Mrs. Santa w/Tray	3,955	1992	$52.95	$95
1992	18 In.	Reindeer w/North Pole	2,755	1992	$63.95	$100
1992	18 In.	Santa w/Banner	6,871	N/A	$52.95	$85
1992	18 In.	Santa w/Cardholder	4,260	1992	$59.95	$90
1992	18 In.	Santa w/Gift List	4,447	N/A	$45.95	$50
1992	18 In.	Santa w/Stocking	3,859	1992	$49.95	$75
1992	18 In.	Santa w/Tray	3,955	N/A	$52.95	$55
1992	18 In.	Snowman w/Broom	4,405	N/A	$46.95	$75
1992	18 In.	Snowy Owl	740	1992	$65.95	$150
1992	18 In.	Witch w/Stand	2,760	1995	$65.95	$100
1992	22 In.	Christmas Stocking	6,128	N/A	$18.45	$40-$45
1992	22 In.	Red Christmas Elf	4,066	1992	$34.95	$60
1992	30 In.	Outdoor Santa	1,724	N/A	$99.95	$125
1992	30 In.	Mrs. Santa w/Cardholder	1,380	N/A	$119.95	$125
1992	30 In.	Santa w/Banner	1,654	N/A	$120.00	$250
1992	30 In.	Santa w/North Pole	1,674	N/A	$109.95	$125-$225
1992	30 In.	Stocking w/Removable 10 In. Elf	2,052	N/A	$27.95	$30
1992	30 In.	Velour Mrs. Santa w/Muff	576	N/A	$160.00	$200
1992	30 In.	Velour Santa w/Pipe & Bag	548	N/A	$160.00	$160-$195
1992	32 In.	Stocking w/Removable 10 In. Elf	2,052	1992	$28.00	$55

Year Introduced	Size (Inches)	Doll	Edition Size	Year Retired	Issue Price	Value
1992	36 In.	Reindeer w/Cardholder	1,219	N/A	$148.00	$225-$295
1993	3 In.	Baby Jesus in Manger	N/A	N/A	$16.95	$40-$50
1993	3 In.	Fishing Santa in Boat	N/A	N/A	$24.95	$25-$35
1993	3 In.	Santa Pin in Card	N/A	N/A	$16.95	$40
1993	5 In.	Baby Jesus in Manger w/Baby	N/A	N/A	$25.95	$50
1993	5 In.	Black Christmas Lamb	N/A	1996	$17.95	$35
1993	5 In.	Christmas Lamb White Fleece	N/A	N/A	$19.50	$35
1993	5 In.	Duck on Flexible Flyer Sled	2,923	N/A	$25.95	$45
1993	5 In.	Easter Parade Boy Duck	N/A	N/A	$21.95	$25
1993	5 In.	Easter Parade Girl Duck	N/A	N/A	$21.95	$45
1993	5 In.	Workshop Elf	N/A	N/A	$13.45	$25
1993	5 In.	Fawn	N/A	N/A	$14.95	$25
1993	5 In.	Leprechaun w/Pot O'Gold	8,775	1996	$15.95	$45
1993	5 In.	Raincoat Duck	N/A	N/A	$22.45	$50
1993	5 In.	Trim a Tree Elf	N/A	N/A	$12.95	$20
1993	7 In.	Angel (Black Hair)	N/A	N/A	$22.95	$45
1993	7 In.	Angel (Blonde Hair)	N/A	1996	$22.95	$40
1993	7 In.	Angel (Brown Hair)	N/A	N/A	$22.95	$45
1993	7 In.	Angel Mouse	N/A	N/A	$21.95	$40
1993	7 In.	Angel w/Musical Instrument	N/A	N/A	$19.95	$30
1993	7 In.	Arab Boy w/Lamb	N/A	1993	$35.95	$80
1993	7 In.	Artist Bunny w/Brush & Palette	N/A	N/A	$20.95	$60
1993	7 In.	Baby New Year (Blonde)	4,127	N/A	$26.95	$55
1993	7 In.	Ballerina Kid (Blonde)	N/A	N/A	$27.95	$55
1993	7 In.	Ballerina on Music Box	N/A	1993	$26.50	$100
1993	7 In.	Bar Mitzvah Boy	N/A	1993	$26.50	$55
1993	7 In.	Baseball Mouse	6,291	N/A	$25.95	$60
1993	7 In.	Basketball Boy (Black)	N/A	1993	$25.95	$50
1993	7 In.	Bedtime Kid	N/A	1993	$25.95	$50
1993	7 In.	Birthday Mouse (Girl)	5,550	N/A	$23.95	$40
1993	7 In.	Boy Building Snowman	N/A	N/A	$21.95	$65
1993	7 In.	Boy Bunny w/Vegetable	5,200	N/A	$20.45	$50
1993	7 In.	Bride Bunny	4,529	N/A	$22.95	$50
1993	7 In.	Bunny in Slipper (Green)	2,550	1993	$19.95	$45
1993	7 In.	Bunny in Slipper (Yellow)	N/A	N/A	$19.95	$45
1993	7 In.	Butterfly Kid (Yellow)	N/A	1994	$27.95	$50
1993	7 In.	Caroler Mouse w/Big Hat & Tree	N/A	N/A	$19.95	$35
1993	7 In.	Champagne Mouse	6,985	N/A	$25.95	$55
1993	7 In.	Chef Santa	N/A	N/A	$28.95	$50
1993	7 In.	Choir Boy	N/A	1995	$25.95	$45
1993	7 In.	Choir Girl	N/A	1995	$25.95	$45
1993	7 In.	Christmas Chicken	N/A	1993	$34.95	$70
1993	7 In.	Christmas Dove	N/A	1995	$27.95	$50
1993	7 In.	Christmas Gnome	N/A	N/A	$18.95	$45
1993	7 In.	Country Boy & Girl Bunny w/Vegetables	N/A	1993	$41.95	$60
1993	7 In.	Country Girl Bunny w/Vegetables	5,621	1993	$20.40	$50
1993	7 In.	Devil Kid	N/A	N/A	$23.95	$55
1993	7 In.	Dracula Kid	N/A	N/A	$25.95	$50
1993	7 In.	Drummer Boy	N/A	1995	$22.45	$40
1993	7 In.	Easter Parade Boy Bunny	N/A	N/A	$20.95	$35

1992 – 5-inch Leprechaun, right, shown standing beside a flower. It wears a dark-green outfit and has a red beard. $25.

1992 – 5-inch Workshop Elf dressed in a red suit and hat. The doll has a blue-and-white striped apron and holds or sits on a gift box. $25.

1992 – 7-inch Angel with Instrument holding a trumpet. The doll has blonde hair and white felt wings. $30.

1992 – 7-inch Artist Bunny wearing blue painter's hat, and a pink-and-blue dress with pink ribbon. The doll has a white body and pink ears, and holds paint and brush. $40.

Year Introduced	Size (Inches)	Doll	Edition Size	Year Retired	Issue Price	Value
1993	7 In.	Easter Parade Girl Bunny	N/A	N/A	$20.95	$35
1993	7 In.	E. P. Girl Bunny w/14 In. Wreath	N/A	1994	$20.95	$50
1993	7 In.	Eric & Shane w/Pin (Signed)	100	1993	$105.00	$425-$750
1993	7 In.	Factory in the Woods Mouse	8,226	1993	$29.95	$55
1993	7 In.	Fireman Mouse	N/A	1993	$25.95	$60
1993	7 In.	Fishing Boy (Black)	N/A	1993	$29.95	$50
1993	7 In.	Free Standing Santa	N/A	N/A	N/A	$30
1993	7 In.	Flower Kid (Yellow & Pink)	N/A	1994	$25.95	$50
1993	7 In.	Flying Angel w/Mistletoe	N/A	N/A	$18.95	$30
1993	7 In.	Ghost Mouse	7,803	1995	$25.95	$55
1993	7 In.	Girl Eating Turkey	N/A	1993	$38.95	$75
1993	7 In.	Habitat Mouse	N/A	1995	$30.95	$55
1993	7 In.	Harvest Basket - Pilgrim Mice	N/A	1996	$47.95	$65
1993	7 In.	Hot Shot Businessman Kid	N/A	1993	$35.95	$40
1993	7 In.	Groom Bunny	3,887	N/A	$22.95	$50
1993	7 In.	Ice Cream Logo w/Pin	17,839	1994	$27.95	$60
1993	7 In.	Indian Boy (Black Hair)	N/A	N/A	$29.95	$50
1993	7 In.	Indian Girl (Black Pony Tails)	N/A	N/A	$29.95	$50
1993	7 In.	Ironing Day Mouse	N/A	1995	$27.95	$40
1993	7 In.	Jump Rope Girl	N/A	1993	$25.95	$50
1993	7 In.	Kid Building Snowman (Blue)	N/A	1993	$21.95	$75
1993	7 In.	Lady Bug Kid	N/A	N/A	$29.95	$45
1993	7 In.	Logo Kid w/Pin	N/A	N/A	$27.50	$50
1993	7 In.	Mouse in Cornucopia	N/A	N/A	$23.95	$45
1993	7 In.	Mouse in Santa's Hat	N/A	N/A	$17.95	$25
1993	7 In.	Mouse on Cheese	N/A	N/A	$26.95	$45
1993	7 In.	Mouse w/Mailbag & Letters	8,000	N/A	$25.95	$45
1993	7 In.	Mouse w/North Pole	N/A	N/A	$21.95	$45
1993	7 In.	Mouse w/Presents (White)	N/A	1994	$21.95	$45
1993	7 In.	Mouse White on Toboggan	N/A	1995	$29.95	$50
1993	7 In.	Mouse w/Snowball	N/A	N/A	$17.95	$35
1993	7 In.	Mr. Ritz Snowman	N/A	N/A	$25.95	$45
1993	7 In.	Mr. Tuckered Mouse	7,059	N/A	$19.95	$35
1993	7 In.	Mr. & Mrs. Victorian Santa	N/A	1993	$59.95	$95
1993	7 In.	Mrs. Santa Candleholder	N/A	N/A	$25.95	$50
1993	7 In.	Mrs. Santa Hanging Merry Christmas Sign	N/A	N/A	$27.95	$40
1993	7 In.	Mrs. Santa w/Poinsettia	N/A	N/A	$29.95	$35
1993	7 In.	Mrs. Santa w/Presents	N/A	N/A	$27.95	$35
1993	7 In.	Mrs. Tuckered Mouse	N/A	N/A	$19.95	$35
1993	7 In.	Pilgrim Boy Hugging Fawn	N/A	1995	$40.95	$75
1993	7 In.	Pilgrim Girl w/Pie	N/A	N/A	$25.95	$65
1993	7 In.	Pilgrim Mice Set w/Basket	N/A	N/A	$46.95	$75
1993	7 In.	Pink Flower Kid	N/A	1993	$25.95	$55
1993	7 In.	Pirate Kid	N/A	N/A	$23.95	$50
1993	7 In.	Santa Bringing Home Christmas Tree	N/A	N/A	$27.95	$45

1992 – 7-inch Baby New Year wearing a diaper and black hat. The doll holds a bell to ring in the New Year 1992. $55.

Year Introduced	Size (Inches)	Doll	Edition Size	Year Retired	Issue Price	Value
1993	7 In.	Santa Candleholder	N/A	N/A	$25.95	$50
1993	7 In.	Santa in Chimney	N/A	N/A	$34.95	$45
1993	7 In.	Santa Skiing	N/A	N/A	$27.95	$45
1993	7 In.	Santa Skunk	N/A	N/A	$27.95	$45
1993	7 In.	Santa w/Dove**	1	N/A	$1,250	$1,250
1993	7 In.	Santa w/Lights	N/A	N/A	$29.95	$60
1993	7 In.	Santa w/Mailbag & Letters	N/A	N/A	$27.95	$50
1993	7 In.	Santa w/Presents	6,996	N/A	$23.95	$30
1993	7 In.	Santa w/Sleigh	N/A	N/A	$39.95	$50
1993	7 In.	Scarecrow Kid	N/A	N/A	$27.95	$50
1993	7 In.	Skiing Santa	N/A	1996	$30.00	$45
1993	7 In.	Snowman (Mr. Ritz)	N/A	N/A	$25.95	$50
1993	7 In.	Snowman (Mrs. Ritz)	N/A	1995	$25.95	$50
1993	7 In.	Snowman on Toboggan	N/A	N/A	$29.95	$55
1993	7 In.	Snowman on Toboggan Carrot Nose	N/A	1995	$29.95	$55
1993	7 In.	Snowman w/Pipe	N/A	N/A	$23.95	$45
1993	7 In.	Snowwoman	N/A	1995	$26.95	$50
1993	7 In.	Spring Boy Rooster	N/A	1993	$34.95	$70
1993	7 In.	Spring Chicken w/Boa	N/A	N/A	$34.95	$60
1993	7 In.	Spring Skunk	N/A	1993	$22.95	$45
1993	7 In.	St. Patrick's Day Mouse	N/A	N/A	$25.95	$35
1993	7 In.	Sweetheart Boy Mouse	N/A	1993	$19.95	$30
1993	7 In.	Sweetheart Girl Mouse	N/A	1993	$19.95	$30
1993	7 In.	Victorian Santa	N/A	1993	$29.95	$55
1993	7 In.	Victorian Santa in Sleigh	N/A	N/A	$59.95	$55-$95
1993	7 In.	White Mouse in Slipper	N/A	N/A	$24.95	$40
1993	7 In.	White Mouse on Toboggan	N/A	N/A	$29.95	$50
1993	7 In.	White Mouse w/Present	N/A	N/A	$21.95	$40
1993	7 In.	White Skating Mouse	N/A	N/A	$24.95	$50
1993	7 In.	Witch Mouse	N/A	1996	$25.95	$40
1993	7 In.	Wizard Mouse	N/A	1995	$27.95	$45
1993	7 In.	Yellow Flower Kid	N/A	N/A	$25.95	$50
1993	8 In.	Boy Turkey	N/A	N/A	$34.95	$75
1993	8 In.	Girl Turkey	N/A	1995	$34.95	$75
1993	10 In.	Angel Bear	N/A	1994	$32.95	$65
1993	10 In.	Baseball Pitcher	N/A	1993	$35.95	$75
1993	10 In.	Baseball Catcher	N/A	1993	$38.50	$75
1993	10 In.	Christa McAuliffe Skier	N/A	N/A	$35.95	$95
1993	10 In.	Christmas Elf (Green)	N/A	N/A	$15.95	$30
1993	10 In.	Christmas Eve Bob Cratchet	N/A	N/A	$69.95	$200
1993	10 In.	Christmas Eve Scrooge	N/A	N/A	$59.95	$200
1993	10 In.	Country Boy Bunny w/Vegetables	N/A	1993	$34.95	$75
1993	10 In.	Country Girl Bunny w/Vegetables	N/A	1993	$34.95	$75
1993	10 In.	Doctor Bear	N/A	1993	$35.95	$90
1993	10 In.	Doe	N/A	N/A	$20.95	$35
1993	10 In.	Easter Parade Boy Bunny	5,139	N/A	$38.95	$65
1993	10 In.	Easter Parade Girl Bunny	6,590	N/A	$38.95	$65
1993	10 In.	Farmer w/Rooster**	1	N/A	$1,000	$1,000
1993	10 In.	Father Time	N/A	N/A	$55	$100
1993	10 In.	Frog in Boat	N/A	N/A	$35.95	$65
1993	10 In.	Gardening Summer Santa	N/A	N/A	$69.95	$115

1992 – 7-inch Beach Kid with Boat wearing blue-and-yellow sun visor hat and blue-and-yellow shorts. It holds a boat. $50.

1992 – 7-inch Drummer Boy (left) and 12-inch Drummer Boy (right). Both are dressed in light-and dark-blue outfits with green scarfs and each plays a drum. $40 for the 7-inch doll; $55 for the 12-inch doll.

1992 – 7-inch Sweetheart Girl Mouse (left) with brown body and pink ears. It wears a white flowered dress and holds a Valentine heart. The 7-inch Sweetheart Boy Mouse (right) has a brown body and pink ears, and holds a pink Valentine heart. $30 each.

1992 – 7-inch Indian Boy with black hair and brown body. It wears a red loincloth, brown vest, white head band, and a red feather in its hair. It has brown shoes and carries a bow and arrow. $50.

1992 – 7-inch Indian Girl with black hair and brown body. It wears a red dress with white trim, white head band and a red feather in her hair. $50.

Year Introduced	Size (Inches)	Doll	Edition Size	Year Retired	Issue Price	Value
1993	10 In.	Gingerbread Boy	N/A	N/A	$22.45	$45
1993	10 In.	Headless Horseman w/Pumpkin Horse	N/A	1994	$56.95	$125-$150
1993	10 In.	Kitten w/Ornament	N/A	1995	$33.95	$60
1993	10 In.	Mrs. Bear in Nightshirt w/Candle	N/A	N/A	$38.95	$75
1993	10 In.	Pony Express Rider	2,500	1994	$97.50	$275
1993	10 In.	Santa w/Fireplace and 3 In. Child	N/A	N/A	$89.95	$150
1993	10 In.	Santa w/Toboggan	N/A	N/A	$59.95	$125
1993	10 In.	Santa's Helper Bear	4,069	1993	$32.95	$70
1993	10 In.	Mrs. Skating Santa	N/A	N/A	$49.95	$95
1993	10 In.	Skating Mr. & Mrs. Santa w/Plaque	N/A	1993	$99.95	$190
1993	10 In.	Snow Queen Tree Topper	N/A	NA	$29.95	$80
1993	10 In.	Snowy Owl	N/A	N/A	$25.95	$60
1993	10 In.	Winter Elf w/14 In. Wreath	N/A	1993	$16.95	$50-$75
1993	12 In.	Chef Santa	N/A	N/A	$44.95	$75
1993	12 In.	Drummer Boy	N/A	1993	$39.95	$55
1993	12 In.	Indian Boy	N/A	1995	$35.95	$80
1993	12 In.	Mrs. Santa w/Poinsettia	N/A	N/A	$49.95	$75
1993	12 In.	Pilgrim Boy w/Basket	N/A	1995	$44.95	$75
1993	12 In.	Pilgrim Girl w/Pie	N/A	N/A	$44.95	$75
1993	12 In.	P. J. Boy	N/A	1993	$29.95	$65
1993	12 In.	P. J. Girl	N/A	N/A	$29.95	$65
1993	12 In.	Santa in Chimney	N/A	N/A	$69.95	$70
1993	12 In.	Santa's Postman w/Cardholder Mailbag	N/A	N/A	$41.00	$75
1993	12 In.	Scarecrow	N/A	N/A	$41.95	$75
1993	12 In.	Snowman	N/A	N/A	$41.95	$75
1993	12 In.	Tuckered Couple	N/A	N/A	$89.95	$125
1993	14 In.	Grapevine Wreath w/7 In. E. P. Girl Bunny	N/A	N/A	$31.95	$50
1993	14 In.	Pumpkin w/Removable Lid	N/A	1995	$49.95	$150
1993	14 In.	Wreath w/Winter Elf	N/A	N/A	$25.95	$50
1993	18 In.	Chef Santa (Pie)	N/A	N/A	$47.95	$130-$150
1993	18 In.	Country Boy Bunny w/Vegetables	N/A	1993	$54.95	$125
1993	18 In.	Country Girl Bunny w/Vegetables	N/A	1993	$54.95	$100
1993	18 In.	Easter Parade Boy Bunny	N/A	N/A	$65.95	$85
1993	18 In.	Easter Parade Girl Bunny	N/A	N/A	$65.95	$95
1993	18 In.	Man Skater (Brown Hair)	N/A	N/A	$44.95	$125
1993	18 In.	Mrs. Outdoor Santa	N/A	N/A	$49.95	$60
1993	18 In.	Mrs. Santa w/Poinsettia	N/A	N/A	$53.95	$70
1993	18 In.	Reindeer w/Christmas Saddlebags	N/A	N/A	$52.95	$95
1993	18 In.	Santa in Sleigh	N/A	N/A	$74.95	$75
1993	18 In.	Santa on Toboggan	N/A	N/A	$69.95	$85
1993	18 In.	Santa w/Banner	N/A	1993	$52.95	$85
1993	18 In.	Santa w/Gift List and Toy Bag	N/A	N/A	$45.95	$55
1993	18 In.	Santa w/Lights	5,441	1993	$54.95	$85
1993	18 In.	Skater Woman	N/A	1993	$44.95	$125
1993	18 In.	Snowman w/Broom	N/A	N/A	$49.95	$75
1993	18 In.	Victorian Mr. Santa	N/A	1998	$64.95	$130-$150
1993	18 In.	Victorian Mrs. Santa	N/A	1997	$64.95	$130-$150
1993	18 In.	Witch Standing	N/A	N/A	$65.95	$100

Year Introduced	Size (Inches)	Doll	Edition Size	Year Retired	Issue Price	Value
1993	22 In.	Christmas Elf	N/A	N/A	$34.95	$60
1993	22 In.	Christmas Stocking	N/A	N/A	$18.45	$40-$45
1993	30 In.	Mrs. Santa w/Cardholder	N/A	N/A	$119.95	$115
1993	30 In.	Santa w/North Pole	N/A	N/A	$129.95	$130
1993	30 In.	Witch Kid	N/A	1995	$149.95	$300
1993	36 In.	Reindeer w/Cardholder	N/A	N/A	$148.45	$225-$295
1994	3 In.	Baby Jesus in Manger	N/A	N/A	$17.50	$40-$50
1994	3 In.	Fishing Santa in Boat	3,048	1994	$24.95	$50
1994	3 In.	Spring Pixie Pick Child	3,557	N/A	$10.95	$45
1994	3 In.	Sun Pick	1,883	N/A	$5.95	$10
1994	3 In.	Sun Pin	7,346	N/A	$5.95	$10
1994	5 In.	Baby Jesus in Manger	1,726	N/A	$26.95	$50
1994	5 In.	Black Christmas Lamb	4,713	N/A	$19.95	$35
1994	5 In.	Christmas Lamb (White Fleece)	7,424	SU	$19.95	$35
1994	5 In.	Caroler Boy (Old World)	7,611	N/A	$19.95	$20
1994	5 In.	Caroler Girl (Old World)	7,817	N/A	$19.95	$20
1994	5 In.	Duck on Flexible Flyer Sled	3,186	1994	$26.95	$45
1994	5 In.	Easter Parade Boy Duck	3,678	N/A	$22.95	$25
1994	5 In.	Easter Parade Girl Duck	4,697	N/A	$24.95	$45
1994	5 In.	Elf (Workshop)	9,416	N/A	$13.95	$25
1994	5 In.	Fawn	8,700	N/A	$14.95	$25
1994	5 In.	Frosty Winter Elf	N/A	1997	$15.50	$25
1994	5 In.	Gold Fall Elf	6,153	N/A	$14.50	$25
1994	5 In.	Green Christmas Elf	8,834	N/A	$13.95	$15
1994	5 In.	Green Spring Elf	3,261	N/A	$13.95	$30
1994	5 In.	Halloween Elf (Black)	N/A	N/A	$14.95	$25
1994	5 In.	Halloween Elf (Orange)	N/A	N/A	$14.95	$25
1994	5 In.	Leprechaun	7,410	N/A	$17.95	$45
1994	5 In.	Old World Caroler Boy	7,611	1995	$19.95	$45
1994	5 In.	Old World Caroler Girl	7,817	1995	$19.95	$45
1994	5 In.	Old World Santa w/9 In. Wreath	2,330	1996	$32.95	$65
1994	5 In.	Orange Fall Elf	6,280	N/A	$14.50	$25-$35
1994	5 In.	Raincoat Duck	2,410	1994	$27.95	$50
1994	5 In.	Red Christmas Elf	11,911	N/A	$13.95	$20-$30
1994	5 In.	Spring Elf w/6 In. Wreath	1,704	1994	$17.95	$55
1994	5 In.	White Christmas Elf	N/A	N/A	$13.95	$25-$30
1994	5 In.	Winter Elf	10,769	N/A	$13.95	$25
1994	5 In.	Yellow Spring Elf	3,932	N/A	$13.95	$35
1994	7 In.	Angel Mouse	10,343	N/A	$22.95	$40
1994	7 In.	Angel w/Musical Instrument	4,302	N/A	$20.95	$30
1994	7 In.	Angel (Black Hair)	2,877	N/A	$23.95	$45
1994	7 In.	Angel (Blonde Hair)	4,584	N/A	$23.95	$40
1994	7 In.	Angel (Brown Hair)	3,362	N/A	$23.95	$45
1994	7 In.	Artist Bunny w/Brush Palette	4,303	N/A	$21.95	$60
1994	7 In.	Auction Times Mouse	5,962	1994	$29.95	$50
1994	7 In.	Baby Bunny w/Bottle	6,588	1995	$19.95	$50
1994	7 In.	Birthday Girl Mouse	3,777	N/A	$23.95	$40
1994	7 In.	Bride Mouse (Signed by Annalee)	4,674	N/A	$22.95	$400
1994	7 In.	Bunny w/Bottle	6,588	N/A	$19.95	$50
1994	7 In.	Butterfly Kid	2,226	1994	$28.95	$50
1994	7 In.	Candy Kiss Kid**	1	N/A	$2,250	$2,200

1992 – 7-inch Mouse with Snowball. The doll has pink ears, black hair and a gray body. It wears a red-and-white cap and outfit and green-and-white scarf. The doll holds a snowball. $35.

1992 – 7-inch Workshop Mouse with gray body, white hair and white beard. It wears green striped clothing and a red hat. It holds a toy train engine and paint brush. $40.

1992 – 10-inch Black Cat with hot pink-and-black ears, black hair and green eyes. The doll wears a green bow. $75.

1992 – 10-inch Christmas Bob Cratchett with brown hair. It wears a cranberry jacket, green pants and black shoes. It holds a quill pen and is seated at its desk. Includes plaque. $200 (signed by Annalee).

Year Introduced	Size (Inches)	Doll	Edition Size	Year Retired	Issue Price	Value
1994	7 In.	Champagne Mouse in Glass	6,360	N/A	$26.95	$55
1994	7 In.	Cheerleader Girl	4,568	1994	$26.95	$45
1994	7 In.	Chef Santa	5,618	N/A	$29.95	$50
1994	7 In.	Choir Boy w/Black Eye	2,912	1995	$26.95	$50
1994	7 In.	Choir Girl (Blonde Hair)	3,424	N/A	$26.95	$45
1994	7 In.	Christa McAuliffe Snowboard Kid	N/A	1994	$39.95	$65
1994	7 In.	Christmas Dove	N/A	N/A	$26.95	$50
1994	7 In.	Clown Mouse**	1	N/A	$1,050	$1,025
1994	7 In.	Cocktail Mouse**	1	N/A	$1,100	$1050
1994	7 In.	Country Boy Bunny w/Hoe	4,842	1994	$21.50	$45
1994	7 In.	Country Girl Bunny w/Basket	6,083	1994	$21.50	$35
1994	7 In.	Dracula Kid	2,126	1994	$26.95	$50
1994	7 In.	Dress Up Santa Logo	20,048	1995	$27.50	$45-$50
1994	7 In.	Drummer Boy	6,817	N/A	$23.95	$40
1994	7 In.	Easter Parade Boy Bunny	9,937	1994	$21.95	$35
1994	7 In.	Easter Parade Girl Bunny	13,186	1994	$21.95	$25
1994	7 In.	Football Mouse	5,998	1994	$29.95	$30
1994	7 In.	Flying Angel	N/A	1996	$19.95	$35
1994	7 In.	Ghost Mouse	4,698	N/A	$26.95	$55
1994	7 In.	Girl Building Snowman (Pink)	13,459	1995	$23.95	$65
1994	7 In.	Girl w/Teddy Bear	4,712	1994	$26.95	$45
1994	7 In.	Graduation Boy Mouse (White Gown)	3,769	1994	$22.95	$40
1994	7 In.	Groom Mouse	N/A	N/A	$22.95	$45
1994	7 In.	Habitat Mouse	5,011	N/A	$29.95	$55
1994	7 In.	Hershey Kid	9,698	1996	$37.50	$65-$75
1994	7 In.	Hot Shot Business Girl	N/A	1994	$36.95	$50
1994	7 In.	Hot Shot Business Girl**	1	1994	$36.95	$450
1994	7 In.	Indian Boy (Black Hair)	2,848	N/A	$30.95	$50

1992 – 7-inch Mr. and Mrs. Tuckered Mouse. Mr. Tuckered Mouse (left) has pink ears and a gray body. It wears a white nightshirt with holly print and holds a hot water bottle. $35. Mrs. Tuckered Mouse (right) has pink ears and a gray body. It wears a white nightshirt with holly print and holds a candle. $35.

1992 – 7-inch Pilgrim Kids with Basket. The Pilgrim Girl wears a white hat, apron and collar over a green-and-white dress. It has black shoes. $85. The Pilgrim Boy wears a green hat, green suit, black shoes and black belt. $85.

Year Introduced	Size (Inches)	Doll	Edition Size	Year Retired	Issue Price	Value
1994	7 In.	Indian Girl (Black Pony Tails)	2,892	N/A	$22.95	$45
1994	7 In.	Jail House Mouse	3,309	1994	$25.95	$45
1994	7 In.	Large Cabbage	778	N/A	$14.95	$45
1994	7 In.	Marbles Kid	N/A	1994	$27.50	$30
1994	7 In.	Mississippi Levee Mouse	3,012	N/A	$29.95	$40
1994	7 In.	Mouse in Cornucopia	6,467	N/A	$24.95	$45
1994	7 In.	Mouse in Santa's Velour Hat	11,641	N/A	$18.50	$25
1994	7 In.	Mouse w/Snowball	8,745	N/A	$18.50	$35
1994	7 In.	Mr. Old World Santa	9,620	N/A	$27.95	$45
1994	7 In.	Mrs. Old World Santa	9,439	N/A	$27.95	$45
1994	7 In.	Mrs. Santa Cardholder	4,443	N/A	$39.95	$40
1994	7 In.	Mrs. Santa w/Fur Trim	8,848	N/A	$22.50	$25
1994	7 In.	Mrs. Santa w/Poinsettia	5,397	1994	$30.95	$35
1994	7 In.	Mrs. Santa w/Presents	5,923	N/A	$28.95	$35
1994	7 In.	Naughty Angel	8,380	N/A	$22.95	$40
1994	7 In.	Pilgrim Boy Hugging Fawn	2,004	N/A	$41.95	$75
1994	7 In.	Pilgrim Girl w/ Pie	2,984	1994	$26.95	$65
1994	7 In.	Pilgrim Mice Set w/Basket	2,873	N/A	$46.95	$75
1994	7 In.	Policeman Mouse	4,788	1994	$27.95	$45
1994	7 In.	Ritz Snowman	4,903	1994	$27.95	$45
1994	7 In.	Santa in Chimney	3,255	1994	$35.95	$45
1994	7 In.	Santa w/Dove**	1	N/A	$1,250	$1,200
1994	7 In.	Santa w/Lights	4,678	N/A	$30.95	$60
1994	7 In.	Santa w/Presents	5,586	N/A	$24.95	$30
1994	7 In.	Santa w/Red Fur Trim Suit	8,922	N/A	$19.95	$30
1994	7 In.	Santa w/Sleigh	3,301	1994	$39.95	$50
1994	7 In.	Santa w/Snowshoe & Tree	8,582	1995	$28.95	$55
1994	7 In.	Santa w/Tree & Sled	8,865	1994	$28.95	$55

1992 – 10-inch Martha Cratchett with Plum Pudding wearing a long flowered dress with pink ribbons and pink shoes. It holds a platter of plum pudding. $150.

1992 – 7-inch Snowman with Pipe (left) wearing a black hat, red scarf and green gloves. It holds a pipe in its mouth and has black boots. $45.
1992 – 7-inch Ritz Snowman (right) wearing a black hat, red-green-and-white outfit, green gloves and black spats. It holds a cane. $45.

1992 – 10-inch Gingerbread Boy with tan body. It wears a red shirt, green jacket trimmed with white rickrack and a green scarf. $45.

1992 – 10-inch Indian Man and Indian Woman. The Indian Man (left) has black hair and wears brown pants, tan moccasins and a red feather in its hair. It holds a bow and arrow. $60. The Indian Woman (right) has black hair and wears a tan dress and tan shoes. It holds an Indian-style blanket. $60.

1992 – 10-inch Reindeer with Cap and Bell (left) wearing a red cap and white tassel. A red bow and bell hang around the doll's neck. It has a tan-and-white body with white ears. $25. A 10-inch Doe is shown at right. $35.

Year Introduced	Size (Inches)	Doll	Edition Size	Year Retired	Issue Price	Value
1994	7 In.	Scottish Lad	3,995	1994	$29.95	$55
1994	7 In.	Snowman w/Pipe	6,179	N/A	$25.95	$45
1994	7 In.	Snowwoman (Mrs. Ritz)	5,344	1994	$26.95	$50
1994	7 In.	St. Patrick Day Mouse	4,746	1996	$26.95	$35
1994	7 In.	Sweetheart Boy Mouse	4,424	1996	$19.95	$30
1994	7 In.	Sweetheart Girl Mouse	N/A	1996	$19.95	$55
1994	7 In.	Thanksgiving Boy	1,881	1994	$39.50	$65
1994	7 In.	Tree Top Star w/3 In. Angel	6,424	1994	$21.00	$40
1994	7 In.	Valentine Girl Kid w/Card	6,220	N/A	$24.95	$45
1994	7 In.	Victorian Santa in Sleigh	1,179	1994	$49.95	$55
1994	7 In.	White Mouse in Slipper	5,838	N/A	$25.95	$40
1994	7 In.	White Mouse on Toboggan	N/A	N/A	$29.95	$50
1994	7 In.	White Mouse w/Present	8,170	N/A	$22.95	$40
1994	7 In.	White Skating Mouse	11,452	N/A	$25.95	$50
1994	7 In.	Witch Mouse	N/A	N/A	$26.95	$40
1994	7 In.	Wizard Mouse	3,892	N/A	$28.95	$45
1994	7 In.	Yellow Flower Kid (Blonde)	2,303	1994	$28.95	$50
1994	8 In.	Boy Turkey	2,852	N/A	$34.95	$75
1994	8 In.	Ear of Corn (no Face)	1,342	N/A	$9.95	$25-$45
1994	8 In.	Girl Turkey	2,174	1994	$34.95	$75
1994	10 In.	Angel Bear	3,337	N/A	$34.50	$65
1994	10 In.	Ballerina Bear**	1	N/A	$1,100	$1,050
1994	10 In.	Baseball Catcher	3,440	1994	$38.50	$75
1994	10 In.	Basketball Player (Black)	2,012	1994	$31.95	$65
1994	10 In.	Basketball Player (White)	3,699	1994	$31.95	$60
1994	10 In.	Bean Nose Santa w/Dome	2,500	N/A	$119.50	$275
1994	10 In.	Boston Bruins Hockey Player	N/A	1995	$47.50	$95
1994	10 In.	Canadian Mountain Horse	N/A	1995	$129.95	$275
1994	10 In.	Canadian Mountie on Horse w/Brass Plaque	N/A	1995	$129.50	$275
1994	10 In.	Christa McAuliffe Ski Doll	N/A	1994	N/A	$100
1994	10 In.	Country Girl Bear**	1	N/A	$925	$925
1994	10 In.	Doe	4,319	N/A	$21.95	$35
1994	10 In.	Easter Parade Boy Bunny	N/A	N/A	$39.95	$65
1994	10 In.	Easter Parade Girl Bunny	N/A	N/A	$39.95	$65
1994	10 In.	Easter Parade Shopper Ostrich	2,368	1994	$33.50	$65
1994	10 In.	Gingerbread Boy	5,182	N/A	$23.50	$45
1994	10 In.	Green Christmas Elf	6,719	N/A	$16.95	$25-$30
1994	10 In.	Headless Horseman w/Pumpkin	1,593	1994	$56.95	$125-$150
1994	10 In.	Hobo Clown	6,826	1994	$30.50	$55-$60
1994	10 In.	Kitten w/Ornament	N/A	1994	$34.95	$60
1994	10 In.	Large Flower w/Face	1,807	1994	$20.95	$50
1994	10 In.	Mrs. Santa Last Mending w/Plaque	5,751	1994	$47.95	$95
1994	10 In.	Old World Caroler Man	5,549	1995	$27.95	$55
1994	10 In.	Old World Caroler Woman	5,595	1995	$27.95	$55
1994	10 In.	Old World Santa w/Skis	4,331	1994	$49.95	$70
1994	10 In.	Old World Skaters on Music Box	1,660	1994	$119.95	$225-$250
1994	10 In.	Piper Bear w/Pin (Signed by Chuck)	200	1994	$129.95	$300
1994	10 In.	Red Christmas Elf	9,079	N/A	$16.95	$25-$30
1994	10 In.	Red Coat w/Cannon	1,000	1994	$79.95	$195
1994	10 In.	Red Coat w/Cannon**	1,500	1994	$79.95	$250

Year Introduced	Size (Inches)	Doll	Edition Size	Year Retired	Issue Price	Value
1994	10 In.	Reindeer w/Cap & Bell	10,319	N/A	$23.95	$25
1994	10 In.	Santa Frog on Bang Hat (Green)	N/A	1994	$29.95	$105
1994	10 In.	Santa Frog on Bang Hat (Red)	N/A	1994	$29.50	$60
1994	10 In.	Skating Penguin	N/A	N/A	$34.95	$60
1994	10 In.	Soccer Player	5,751	1994	$34.95	$60
1994	10 In.	Tree Top Angel	N/A	N/A	$29.95	$60
1994	10 In.	White Christmas Elf	N/A	N/A	$16.95	$30
1994	10 In.	White St. Nicholas	5,560	N/A	$43.95	$95
1994	10 In.	Window Shopper Ostrich	N/A	N/A	$37.95	$50
1994	10 In.	Winter Elf	8,504	N/A	$17.50	$30
1994	12 In.	Bean Nose Santa w/Brass Plaque	N/A	1995	$119.50	$225-$275
1994	12 In.	Boy Pilgrim w/Basket	2,132	N/A	$23.00	$65
1994	12 In.	Cat Kid	N/A	1995	$36.50	$75
1994	12 In.	Chef Santa	1,519	N/A	$45.95	$75
1994	12 In.	Devil Kid	2,610	1994	$39.95	$75
1994	12 In.	Drummer Boy	3,792	N/A	$39.95	$55
1994	12 In.	Girl Cat Kid	3,176	N/A	$35.95	$70
1994	12 In.	Girl Pilgrim w/Pie	2,140	N/A	$45.95	$95
1994	12 In.	Girl Scarecrow (Blue Stoned Wash Dress)	3,978	1995	$47.95	$75
1994	12 In.	Mrs. Santa Cardholder	4,443	N/A	$39.95	$65
1994	12 In.	North Pole w/Red Ribbon Wrap	1,561	N/A	$9.50	$20
1994	12 In.	Santa in Chimney	668	N/A	$69.95	$75
1994	14 In.	Grapevine Wreath w/Girl Bunny	2,505	N/A	$34.95	$50-$75
1994	14 In.	Large Pumpkin	2,486	N/A	$49.95	$150
1994	17 In.	Tee Pee	1,838	1996	$36.95	$65
1994	18 In.	Chef Santa	2,888	N/A	$49.95	$105-$125
1994	18 In.	Country Boy Bunny w/Hoe	1,260	N/A	$56.95	$95
1994	18 In.	Country Girl Bunny w/Basket	1,549	N/A	$65.50	$95
1994	18 In.	Easter Parade Boy Bunny	2,019	N/A	$65.50	$85
1994	18 In.	Easter Parade Girl Bunny	2,299	N/A	$65.50	$85
1994	18 In.	Indoor Santa w/Lights	3,785	N/A	$65.50	$95
1994	18 In.	Mr. Fur Santa	N/A	N/A	$45.95	$75
1994	18 In.	Mr. Fur Santa on Stand	4,546	N/A	$45.95	$75
1994	18 In.	Mr. Old World Santa	N/A	N/A	$52.00	$85
1994	18 In.	Mrs. Old World Santa	5,278	N/A	$50.00	$85
1994	18 In.	Mrs. Outdoor Santa	3,614	N/A	$49.95	$60
1994	18 In.	Mrs. Santa Cardholder	4,312	N/A	$52.95	$55
1994	18 In.	Mrs. Santa w/Poinsettia	2,992	1994	$55.95	$70
1994	18 In.	Musical Mrs. Santa	1,498	N/A	$59.95	$85-$125
1994	18 In.	Musical Santa Gift List	1,316	N/A	$59.95	$95-$125
1994	18 In.	Old World Reindeer w/Bells	5,201	1995	$59.95	$95-$110
1994	18 In.	P. J. Kid w/2 Christmas Stockings	2,428	N/A	$59.95	$95
1994	18 In.	Reindeer w/Christmas Saddlebags	3,235	1994	$54.95	$85-$95
1994	18 In.	Santa in Sleigh	1,140	1994	$77.95	$80
1994	18 In.	Santa on Toboggan	1,499	N/A	$69.95	$80
1994	18 In.	Santa w/Cardholder Sack	4,899	N/A	$54.95	$75
1994	18 In.	Snowman w/Broom	4,092	N/A	$49.95	$75
1994	18 In.	Witch	1,823	N/A	$67.95	$95
1994	22 In.	Christmas Elf (Black Hair)	3,606	N/A	$34.95	$60
1994	22 In.	Christmas Stocking	6,796	N/A	$18.95	$40-$50

1992 – 10-inch Skaters (Man and Woman). The Man Skater (left) wears a long burgundy coat, black top hat and gray gloves. $85. The Woman Skater (right) wears a long blue and green coat with white fur, burgundy gloves and a white hat. $85.

1992 – 12-inch Pilgrim Girl Mouse (left) and Boy Mouse (right). The Girl Mouse wears a white hat and green checkered dress. It has pink ears. $85. The Boy Mouse wears a green top hat, green jacket and black belt. It has pink ears with a gray body. $85.

1992 – 12-inch Santa with Potbelly Stove. It has white hair and a white beard. The doll wears a dark green-and-ivory vest, white shirt, red pants and green shoes. Its back is toward the potbelly stove. $85.

1992 – 10-inch Country Girl Bunny with Flowers (left) and a Country Boy Bunny (right). Each wears the same color pastel plaid outfit, and has white hair and pink ears. The boy bunny holds a butterfly. Both are standing on a green base. $55 each.

1992 – 10-inch Easter Parade Girl Bunny (right) and Boy Bunny (left). The Girl Bunny wears a navy blue-and-white Easter outfit, navy blue hat and black shoes. It holds an umbrella. $65. The Boy Bunny wears a white top hat, Easter outfit with navy blue-and-white jacket and black necktie. It holds a white cane. $65.

1992 – 12-inch Santa's Helper Painting Boat (right), paint brush and boat in hand and a 12-inch Santa's Postman (left) sitting in Santa's mailbag. Santa's Helper is $65; Santa's Postman is $75.

Year Introduced	Size (Inches)	Doll	Edition Size	Year Retired	Issue Price	Value
1994	24 In.	Turkey	1,116	1994	$99.95	$300
1994	30 In.	Country Girl Bunny w/Basket	722	N/A	$119.95	$200-$250
1994	30 In.	Mr. Old World Santa	1,453	N/A	$124.95	$250
1994	30 In.	Mrs. Old World Santa	1,410	N/A	$124.95	$250
1994	30 In.	Outdoor Santa w/Toy Bag	1,019	N/A	$125.95	$130
1994	30 In.	Santa w/Cardholder Sack	1,148	N/A	$119.95	$125
1994	30 In.	Santa w/North Pole Suit	643	N/A	$131.95	$135-$225
1994	30 In.	Snowman w/Broom	1,782	1995	$119.95	$275-$295
1994	30 In.	Witch Kid	722	N/A	$149.95	$300
1994	36 In.	Reindeer w/Cardholder Saddlebags	902	N/A	$148.45	$225-$295
1994	48 In.	Quilted Tree Skirt	N/A	N/A	$24.95	$45-$55
1995	2 In.	Cactus Set	N/A	N/A	$59.50	$100
1995	2 In.	Pumpkin	N/A	1996	$6.95	$20-$25
1995	2 In.	Tomatoes w/Face 3	N/A	1996	$12.95	$35
1995	3 In.	Baby Jesus in Manger	N/A	N/A	$17.95	$40-$50
1995	3 In.	Christmas Morn Itsie Vignette (Signed by Chuck Thorndike)	N/A	1995	$67.95	$150
1995	3 In.	Musical Ballooning Kids	N/A	N/A	$55.95	$85
1995	3 In.	Spring Pixie Pick	N/A	N/A	$11.50	$45
1995	3 In.	Sun Pin	N/A	N/A	$5.95	$10
1995	3 In.	Sweetheart Itsie Boy Mouse	N/A	N/A	$14.95	$35
1995	3 In.	Sweetheart Itsie Girl Mouse	N/A	N/A	$14.95	$35
1995	3 In.	Wynken, Blynken, Nod	N/A	1996	$67.95	$100
1995	3 In.	Witch Kid w/Broom	N/A	N/A	$17.95	$35
1995	3 In.	Witch w/Halloween Moon Mobile	N/A	1996	$44.95	$115
1995	5 In.	Angel w/18 In. Christmas Moon (Yellow)	N/A	1995	$54.95	$95
1995	5 In.	Angel w/Mistletoe	N/A	N/A	$16.50	$30
1995	5 In.	Baby Jesus in Manger w/Hay	N/A	N/A	$27.50	$50
1995	5 In.	Black Christmas Lamb	N/A	N/A	$20.50	$35
1995	5 In.	Boudoir Baby w/Blanket	N/A	N/A	$19.95	$45
1995	5 In.	Cactus Set (And 12 In.)	N/A	1996	$17.95	$45
1995	5 In.	Easter Parade Boy Duck	N/A	N/A	$25.50	$25
1995	5 In.	Easter Parade Girl Duck	N/A	N/A	$25.50	$25
1995	5 In.	Elk Workshop	N/A	N/A	$14.50	$15
1995	5 In.	Fawn	N/A	N/A	$15.50	$25
1995	5 In.	Gold Fall Elf w/Leaf	N/A	N/A	$14.95	$35
1995	5 In.	Green Christmas Elf	N/A	N/A	$14.50	$20
1995	5 In.	Green Spring Elf	N/A	N/A	$14.50	$30
1995	5 In.	Halloween Elf (Black)	N/A	N/A	$15.50	$25
1995	5 In.	Halloween Elf (Orange)	N/A	N/A	$15.50	$25
1995	5 In.	Leprechaun w/Pot O'Gold	N/A	N/A	$19.95	$45
1995	5 In.	Old World Caroler Boy	N/A	N/A	$20.50	$45
1995	5 In.	Old World Caroler Girl	N/A	N/A	$20.50	$45
1995	5 In.	Old World Santa w/9 In. Wreath	N/A	N/A	$33.95	$65
1995	5 In.	Orange Fall Elf w/Leaf	N/A	N/A	$14.95	$30
1995	5 In.	Pixie Piccolo Player	35	1996	$29.95	$40
1995	5 In.	Red Christmas Elf	N/A	N/A	$14.50	$20
1995	5 In.	Sailor Duck	N/A	1996	$25.50	$55
1995	5 In.	White Christmas Elf	N/A	N/A	$14.50	$25
1995	5 In.	White Christmas Lamb	N/A	N/A	$20.50	$35

Year Introduced	Size (Inches)	Doll	Edition Size	Year Retired	Issue Price	Value
1995	5 In.	Winter Elf	N/A	N/A	$14.50	$25
1995	5 In.	Yellow Spring Elf	N/A	N/A	$14.50	$30
1995	7 In.	Angel (Black Hair)	N/A	N/A	$24.50	$45
1995	7 In.	Angel (Blonde Hair)	N/A	N/A	$24.50	$40
1995	7 In.	Angel (Brown Hair)	N/A	N/A	$24.50	$45
1995	7 In.	Angel Mouse	N/A	N/A	$23.50	$40
1995	7 In.	Angel w/Musical Instrument	N/A	N/A	$21.50	$30
1995	7 In.	Angel Playing Harp	N/A	1996	$26.95	$45
1995	7 In.	Artist Bunny w/Brush & Palette	N/A	N/A	$22.50	$60
1995	7 In.	Baby Bunny w/Baby Bottle	N/A	N/A	$20.50	$50
1995	7 In.	Bicyclist Boy Mouse	N/A	N/A	$25.95	$40
1995	7 In.	Birthday Girl Mouse	N/A	N/A	$24.50	$40
1995	7 In.	Bride Mouse	N/A	N/A	$23.50	$45
1995	7 In.	California Mudslide Mouse	N/A	1995	$29.95	$50
1995	7 In.	Caroler Mouse w/Big Hat & Tree	N/A	N/A	$21.50	$35
1995	7 In.	Champagne Mouse in Glass	N/A	N/A	$27.50	$55
1995	7 In.	Cheerleader Mouse	N/A	N/A	$12.00	$75
1995	7 In.	Chef Mouse w/Wisk Bowl	N/A	1995	$27.50	$60
1995	7 In.	Chef Santa	N/A	N/A	$30.50	$50
1995	7 In.	Choir Boy	N/A	N/A	$27.50	$45
1995	7 In.	Choir Boy w/Black Eye	N/A	N/A	$27.50	$50
1995	7 In.	Choir Girl	N/A	N/A	$27.50	$45
1995	7 In.	Christmas Dove	N/A	N/A	$27.50	$50
1995	7 In.	Christmas Party Girl Mouse	N/A	N/A	$18.95	$25
1995	7 In.	Country Boy Bunny w/Apple	N/A	N/A	$24.50	$50
1995	7 In.	Easter Bunny Kid w/Basket	N/A	1996	$22.50	$55
1995	7 In.	Flying Angel	N/A	N/A	$21.95	$35
1995	7 In.	Garden Club Mouse	N/A	N/A	$22.50	$35
1995	7 In.	Ghost Mouse	N/A	N/A	$27.50	$55
1995	7 In.	Girl Building a Snowman	N/A	N/A	$24.95	$65
1995	7 In.	Goin' Fishin Logo	18,575	1995	$29.95	$45
1995	7 In.	Graduation Boy Mouse	N/A	N/A	$24.50	$40
1995	7 In.	Graduation Girl Mouse	N/A	N/A	$24.50	$45
1995	7 In.	Groom Mouse	N/A	N/A	$23.50	$45
1995	7 In.	Gypsy Girl Kid	N/A	1996	$31.95	$55
1995	7 In.	Habitat Mouse	N/A	N/A	$30.50	$65
1995	7 In.	Hershey Kid	N/A	N/A	$38.50	$65
1995	7 In.	Hockey Kid	N/A	1995	$30.95	$50
1995	7 In.	Holly Girl Mouse	N/A	N/A	$18.95	$25
1995	7 In.	Housewife Mouse	N/A	N/A	$25.95	$65
1995	7 In.	Indian Boy Kid w/Spear	N/A	N/A	$29.95	$50
1995	7 In.	Indian Girl Kid w/Beads	N/A	N/A	$29.95	$60
1995	7 In.	Joseph Child	N/A	1995	$28.95	$65
1995	7 In.	Large Cabbage	N/A	N/A	$17.95	$45
1995	7 In.	Marbles Kid	N/A	N/A	$27.50	$65
1995	7 In.	Mary Child w/Doll	N/A	1995	$28.95	$85
1995	7 In.	Mikey the Bikey	N/A	N/A	$30.95	$35
1995	7 In.	Motorcycle Mouse	N/A	N/A	$30.95	$50
1995	7 In.	Mouse in Cornucopia	N/A	N/A	$25.50	$45
1995	7 In.	Mouse in Santa's Hat	N/A	N/A	$18.95	$25
1995	7 In.	Mouse Kid	N/A	1996	$22.50	$45

1992 – 12-inch Mrs. Santa with Poinsettias & 12-inch Chef Santa. Mrs. Santa (left) wears a white hat, white apron, dark green-and-ivory full-length dress, and holds a poinsettia. $75. The Chef Santa (right) has white hair and beard, and wears a white chef's hat and white apron. It also has a red outfit and green gloves. $75.

1992 – 12-inch Tuckered Couple. Mr. Tuckered is dressed in a red-and-white robe and green shoes. It holds a hot-water bottle. Mrs. Tuckered wears a red robe and green shoes. It holds a candle. $125 each.

1992 – 18-inch Bunny Kid with Slippers wears a white Bunny suit and pink-and-white slippers. $95.

Year Introduced	Size (Inches)	Doll	Edition Size	Year Retired	Issue Price	Value
1995	7 In.	Mouse w/Snowball	N/A	N/A	$18.95	$35
1995	7 In.	Mr. & Mrs. Indoor Santa w/Tree	N/A	N/A	$69.95	$70
1995	7 In.	Mr. Old World Santa	N/A	N/A	$28.95	$45
1995	7 In.	Mrs. Santa w/Fur Trim	N/A	N/A	$23.95	$25
1995	7 In.	Mrs. Santa w/Presents	N/A	N/A	$30.95	$35
1995	7 In.	Nashville Boy	N/A	1995	$29.95	$60
1995	7 In.	Nashville Girl	N/A	1995	$29.95	$60
1995	7 In.	Naughty Angel w/Black Eye	N/A	N/A	$25.95	$50
1995	7 In.	Pilgrim Boy w/Fawn	2,004	N/A	$41.95	$65
1995	7 In.	Pilgrim Girl w/Pie	N/A	N/A	$26.95	$75
1995	7 In.	Pilgrim Mice Set w/Basket	N/A	N/A	$47.95	$65
1995	7 In.	P. J. Kid on Rocking Horse	N/A	SU	$29.95	$55
1995	7 In.	Santa	N/A	N/A	$20.50	$25
1995	7 In.	Santa Hugging Reindeer	N/A	N/A	$47.95	$50
1995	7 In.	Santa Mouse in Chimney	N/A	N/A	$34.95	$50
1995	7 In.	Santa Skiing	N/A	N/A	$29.95	$45
1995	7 In.	Santa w/Lights	N/A	N/A	$31.95	$60
1995	7 In.	Santa w/North Pole	N/A	N/A	$35.95	$40
1995	7 In.	Santa w/Presents	N/A	N/A	$27.95	$30
1995	7 In.	Santa w/Sleigh	N/A	N/A	$39.95	$50
1995	7 In.	Santa w/Snowshoes & Tree	N/A	N/A	$29.95	$55
1995	7 In.	Santa Indoor	N/A	N/A	$19.95	$20
1995	7 In.	Shepherd Child w/Lamb	N/A	1995	$39.95	$85
1995	7 In.	Snowman on Toboggan	N/A	N/A	$30.95	$55
1995	7 In.	Snowman w/Pipe	N/A	N/A	$26.50	$45
1995	7 In.	Snowwoman (Mrs. Ritz)	N/A	N/A	$27.50	$50
1995	7 In.	South American Girl	N/A	1995	$31.95	$50
1995	7 In.	St. Patrick's Day Mouse	N/A	N/A	$26.95	$35
1995	7 In.	Sweetheart Boy Mouse	N/A	N/A	$20.95	$30
1995	7 In.	Sweetheart Girl Mouse	N/A	N/A	$20.95	$30

1992 – 18-inch Mrs. Santa with Presents wearing a green and ivory dress, white hat, white apron and black shoes. It holds Christmas presents. $70.

1992 – 22-inch Red Christmas Elf dressed in a red suit with red fur trim. The doll has a red hat with white pompom. $60.

1992 – 12-inch Spider (left) with black legs, orange hair, orange nose and multi-colored feet. The doll wears a green top hat. $75. 12-inch Bat (right) has a white body and black wings. It wears a green tie and carries a trick-or-treat bag. $75.

Year Introduced	Size (Inches)	Doll	Edition Size	Year Retired	Issue Price	Value
1995	7 In.	Swiss Alps Boy	N/A	1995	$31.95	$50
1995	7 In.	Tree Top Mouse in Chimney	N/A	N/A	$34.95	$50
1995	7 In.	Tree Top Star w/3 In. Angel	N/A	N/A	$21.50	$65
1995	7 In.	Valentine Girl Kid w/Card	N/A	N/A	$26.95	$45
1995	7 In.	White Mouse in Slipper	N/A	N/A	$26.50	$40
1995	7 In.	White Mouse on Toboggan w/Present	N/A	N/A	$30.95	$50
1995	7 In.	White Skating Mouse	N/A	N/A	$26.50	$50
1995	7 In.	Witch Mouse	3,009	N/A	$27.50	$40
1995	7 In.	Wizard Mouse	N/A	N/A	$29.50	$45
1995	8 In.	Boy Turkey	N/A	N/A	$35.50	$75
1995	8 In.	Ear of Corn	N/A	N/A	$12.95	$45
1995	8 In.	Easter Parade Boy Bunny	N/A	N/A	$27.95	$65
1995	8 In.	Easter Parade Girl Bunny	N/A	N/A	$27.95	$65
1995	8 In.	Girl Turkey	N/A	N/A	$35.50	$75
1995	10 In.	Boston Bruins Hockey Player	N/A	1995	$47.50	$95
1995	10 In.	Boston Bruins Hockey Player (Signed by Chuck Thorndike & S. Leech)	N/A	1995	$57.50	$150
1995	10 In.	Canadian Mounty	N/A	1995	$74.95	$150
1995	10 In.	Canadian Mounty w/Horse	N/A	1995	$129.95	$275
1995	10 In.	Chip Bear in Boat w/Pin (Signed by Chuck Thorndike)	200	1995	$125.00	$300
1995	10 In.	Christmas Elf	N/A	N/A	$18.00	$25-$30
1995	10 In.	Collector Mr. Santa w/Wee Helper	N/A	N/A	$74.95	$125
1995	10 In.	Collector Mrs. Nashville Santa	N/A	N/A	$44.95	$90
1995	10 In.	Doe	N/A	N/A	$22.50	$35
1995	10 In.	Easter Parade Boy Bunny	N/A	N/A	$40.95	$65
1995	10 In.	Easter Parade Girl Bunny	N/A	N/A	$40.95	$65
1995	10 In.	Frog on Lily Pad	N/A	N/A	$23.95	$50
1995	10 In.	Green Christmas Elf	N/A	N/A	$17.50	$25-$30

1993 – 7-inch Artist Bunny with pink ears. The doll wears a pink outfit and large blue hat. A blue ribbon holds the doll's paint brush and artist palette. $60.

1993 – 7-inch Basketball Boy with black hair. It wears a white short-sleeve shirt, hot pink shorts and black sneakers. It holds a basketball. $50.

1993 – 5-inch Easter Parade Boy and Girl Ducks. The Boy Duck (left) has a yellow body, orange legs and white hat. $25. The Girl Duck (right) has a yellow body, orange legs and a floral hat. It holds a pink purse. $45.

1993 – 7-inch Fishing Boy with black hair. He holds a fishing pole and sits on a dock. $50.

1993 – 7-inch Mouse with Mailbag wearing a red hat, white ear muffs and green scarf. It holds a U. S. mailbag with letters. $45.

Year Introduced	Size (Inches)	Doll	Edition Size	Year Retired	Issue Price	Value
1995	10 In.	Indian Chief & Maiden	N/A	1996	$85.50	$160
1995	10 In.	Indian Chief & Maiden	N/A	1996	$85.50	$160
1995	10 In.	Indian Man	N/A	1996	$42.95	$80
1995	10 In.	Indian Woman	N/A	N/A	$42.95	$75
1995	10 In.	Kitten w/Ornament	N/A	N/A	$35.95	$60
1995	10 In.	Large Flower w/Face	N/A	N/A	$20.95	$50
1995	10 In.	Old World Caroler Man	N/A	N/A	$28.95	$55
1995	10 In.	Old World Caroler Woman	N/A	N/A	$27.95	$55
1995	10 In.	Pocahontas w/Dome	1,300	1996	$87.50	$275
1995	10 In.	Red Christmas Elf	N/A	N/A	$17.50	$25-$30
1995	10 In.	Red Tree Top Angel	N/A	N/A	$35.95	$40
1995	10 In.	Redcoat w/Cannon	1,000	N/A	$79.95	$195-$250
1995	10 In.	Reindeer	N/A	N/A	$23.95	$25
1995	10 In.	Reindeer w/7 In. Santa	N/A	N/A	$47.95	$75
1995	10 In.	Reindeer w/Cap & Bell	N/A	N/A	$24.95	$25
1995	10 In.	Skating Penguin	N/A	N/A	$35.95	$60
1995	10 In.	Tennessee Fiddler**	N/A	$1995	$79.95	$175
1995	10 In.	Tree Top Angel	N/A	N/A	$35.95	$55
1995	10 In.	Valentine Girl Bear	2,487	N/A	$35.95	$60
1995	10 In.	White Christmas Elf	N/A	N/A	$17.50	$30
1995	10 In.	White St. Nicholas	N/A	N/A	$44.95	$95
1995	10 In.	Window Shopper Ostrich	N/A	N/A	$38.95	$50
1995	10 In.	Winter Elf	N/A	N/A	$17.95	$30
1995	12 In.	Boy Pilgrim w/Basket	N/A	N/A	$46.95	$65
1995	12 In.	Cactus Set	N/A	N/A	$17.95	$45
1995	12 In.	Chef Santa	N/A	N/A	$46.95	$75
1995	$12 In.	Drummer Boy	N/A	N/A	$39.95	$55
1995	12 In.	Empress the Carousel Horse (1st in Series)	N/A	1996	$61.95	$100-$150
1995	12 In.	Girl Cat Kid	N/A	N/A	$36.95	$70
1995	12 In.	Girl Pilgrim w/Pie	N/A	N/A	$46.95	$95
1995	12 In.	Girl Scarecrow	N/A	N/A	$48.95	$75
1995	12 Inches	Mr. Indoor Santa w/Tree Top Star	N/A	N/A	$49.95	$75
1995	12 In.	Mrs. Indoor Santa w/Garland	N/A	N/A	$44.95	$85
1995	12 In.	Mrs. Santa Cardholder	N/A	N/A	$43.95	$65
1995	12 In.	North Pole	N/A	N/A	$9.95	$20
1995	12 In.	Old World St. Nicholas	N/A	N/A	$54.95	$75
1995	12 In.	Rose & Ivy Arbor	N/A	N/A	$49.95	$75
1995	12 In.	Santa in Chimney	N/A	N/A	$71.95	$75
1995	14 In.	Large Pumpkin w/Removable Top	N/A	N/A	$49.95	$150
1995	17 In.	Teepee	N/A	N/A	$37.95	$65
1995	18 In.	Chef Santa	N/A	N/A	$51.95	$105-$150
1995	18 In.	Country Boy Bunny w/Apple	N/A	N/A	$67.50	$90
1995	18 In.	Country Girl Bunny w/Apple	N/A	N/A	$67.50	$95
1995	18 In.	Easter Parade Boy Bunny	N/A	N/A	$67.50	$90
1995	18 In.	Easter Parade Girl Bunny	N/A	N/A	$67.50	$90
1995	18 In.	Indoor Santa w/Lights	N/A	N/A	$63.95	$95
1995	18 In.	Mr. Fur Santa on Stand	N/A	N/A	$46.95	$60
1995	18 In.	Mr. Indoor Santa w/Tree Top Star	N/A	N/A	$59.95	$85
1995	18 In.	Mr. Old World Santa	N/A	N/A	$53.00	$85
1995	18 In.	Mrs. Indoor Santa w/Garland	N/A	N/A	$54.95	$80

Year Introduced	Size (Inches)	Doll	Edition Size	Year Retired	Issue Price	Value
1995	18 In.	Mrs. Old World Santa	N/A	N/A	$51.00	$85
1995	18 In.	Mrs. Outdoor Santa	N/A	N/A	$51.00	$60
1995	18 In.	Mrs. Santa Cardholder	N/A	N/A	$53.95	$55
1995	18 In.	Musical Santa w/Gift List	N/A	N/A	$61.95	$95
1995	18 In.	Old World Reindeer w/Bells	N/A	N/A	$61.95	$95
1995	18 In.	P. J. Kid in 2 Foot Stocking	N/A	N/A	$61.95	$95-$125
1995	18 In.	Reindeer w/Christmas Saddlebags	N/A	N/A	$55.95	$85
1995	18 In.	Reindeer w/Santa	N/A	N/A	$89.95	$90
1995	18 In.	Santa on Toboggan	N/A	N/A	$73.95	$80
1995	18 In.	Santa Hugging Reindeer	N/A	N/A	$89.95	$90
1995	18 In.	Santa w/Cardholder	N/A	N/A	$59.95	$75
1995	18 In.	Santa w/Gift List & Toy Bag	N/A	N/A	$49.95	$55
1995	18 In.	Snowman w/Broom	N/A	N/A	$51.95	$75
1995	18 In.	Witch w/Stand	N/A	N/A	$69.95	$100
1995	22 In.	Christmas Stocking	N/A	N/A	$19.50	$45-$50
1995	22 In.	Green Christmas Elf	N/A	N/A	$35.95	$75
1995	22 In.	Red Christmas Elf	N/A	N/A	$35.95	$60
1995	30 In.	Country Boy Bunny w/Apples	N/A	N/A	$124.95	$210
1995	30 In.	Mr. Old World Santa	N/A	N/A	$124.95	$225-$300
1995	30 In.	Mrs. Old World Santa	N/A	N/A	$124.95	$225-$300
1995	30 In.	Mrs. Santa w/Cardholder Apron	N/A	N/A	$119.95	$125
1995	30 In.	Outdoor Santa w/Toy Bag	N/A	N/A	$137.95	$140
1995	30 In.	Santa w/Cardholder Sack	N/A	N/A	$119.95	$125
1995	30 In.	Santa w/North Pole	N/A	N/A	$137.95	$125-$225
1995	30 In.	Snowman	N/A	N/A	$119.95	$275-$295
1995	30 In.	Witch Kid	N/A	N/A	$149.95	$300
1995	36 In.	Reindeer w/Cardholder Saddlebags	N/A	N/A	$154.50	$225-$295
1995	48 In.	Tree Skirt	N/A	N/A	$29.95	$45
1996	2 In.	Pumpkin w/Face	N/A	N/A	$7.00	$20-$25
1996	2 In.	Red Tomatoes (Set of 3)	N/A	1996	$13.50	$35
1996	3 In.	Birthday Mouse	N/A	N/A	$21.00	$35
1996	3 In.	Bride Mouse	N/A	1996	$24.00	$35
1996	3 In.	Butterfly Pick	N/A	1996	$15.00	$35
1996	3 In.	Butterfly Pin	N/A	1996	$15.00	$35
1996	3 In.	Canoeing Indian Kids	N/A	N/A	$39.50	$60
1996	3 In.	Caroling Boy	8,036	N/A	$17.50	$35
1996	3 In.	Caroling Girl	8,034	N/A	$21.50	$45
1996	3 In.	Computer Mouse	N/A	1996	$21.50	$45
1996	3 In.	Dreams of Gold Vignette w/Dome	N/A	1996	$84.50	$115
1996	3 In.	Easter Bunny	N/A	N/A	$19.50	$35
1996	3 In.	Froggie	N/A	1996	$13.50	$40
1996	3 In.	Ghost Mouse	N/A	1998	$21.50	$50
1996	3 In.	Groom Mouse	N/A	N/A	$22.00	$35
1996	3 In.	Hershey Boy Mouse	N/A	N/A	$23.00	$55
1996	3 In.	Hershey Girl Mouse	N/A	1996	$23.00	$55
1996	3 In.	Hiker Mouse	N/A	1996	$25.00	$45
1996	3 In.	Indian Boy	N/A	N/A	$20.00	$40
1996	3 In.	Indian Girl	N/A	N/A	$20.00	$40
1996	3 In.	Lady Bug Pick	N/A	1997	$15.00	$30
1996	3 In.	Mailman Mouse	N/A	1996	$21.50	$50
1996	3 In.	Matchbox Mice	N/A	N/A	$33.50	$50

1993 – 10-inch Baseball Pitcher wearing a blue sun visor cap, white-and-blue uniform, blue/white striped leggings and blue shoes. It has a baseball and glove, and is pitching. $75.

1993 – 10-inch Gardening Summer Santa with white hair and white beard. It wears a red plaid long-sleeve shirt, blue bib overalls and tan boots. The doll holds a hoe and is wiping his forehead. It stands on a platform with garden vegetables. $115.

93

1993 – 10-inch Santa with Fireplace and 3-inch Child. Santa stands by fireplace holding a green bag. A little girl and gifts are setting on the platform. Includes plaque. $150 (signed by Annalee).

1993 – 12-inch Drummer Boy wearing white hat, white jacket, red pants and white boots. It has a green scarf and is playing drum. $55.

Year Introduced	Size (Inches)	Doll	Edition Size	Year Retired	Issue Price	Value
1996	3 In.	Musical Ballooning Bears	N/A	1996	$59.50	$85
1996	3 In.	Nurse Mouse	N/A	N/A	$21.50	$40
1996	3 In.	Pilgrim Boy	N/A	N/A	$21.50	$40
1996	3 In.	Pilgrim Girl Itsie Series	N/A	N/A	$21.50	$40
1996	3 In.	Sleigh Ride Santa	N/A	N/A	$23.50	$30
1996	3 In.	Teachers Mouse	N/A	1997	$20.00	$35
1996	3 In.	Witch w/Broom	N/A	N/A	$18.50	$35
1996	3 In.	Witch w/Halloween Moon Mobile	N/A	N/A	$44.50	$115
1996	3 In.	Wizard Mouse	N/A	1996	$23.50	$40
1996	3 In.	Wynken, Blynken & Nod	N/A	1996	$67.50	$100
1996	3 In.	Yellow Duckling	N/A	N/A	$21.00	$40
1996	4 In.	Angel w/Mistletoe	N/A	N/A	$17.50	$30
1996	4 In.	Puppy Present	N/A	1997	$20.50	$35
1996	4 In.	Street Lamp	N/A	N/A	$7.50	$10
1996	5 In.	Angel Centerpiece	N/A	N/A	$30.50	$60
1996	5 In.	Angel w/Mistletoe	N/A	1996	$17.50	$30
1996	5 In.	Black Christmas Lamb	N/A	N/A	$17.50	$45
1996	5 In.	Blanket Baby Boy	N/A	1996	$20.00	$45
1996	5 In.	Blanket Baby Girl	N/A	1996	$20.00	$45
1996	5 In.	Cactus Set	N/A	N/A	$23.50	$45
1996	5 In.	Elf Centerpiece	N/A	N/A	$26.50	$55
1996	5 In.	Elf Fawn	N/A	N/A	$15.50	$25
1996	5 In.	Elf Workshop	N/A	N/A	N/A	$25
1996	5 In.	Green Christmas Elf	N/A	N/A	$14.50	$20
1996	5 In.	Halloween Elf (Black)	N/A	N/A	$14.50	$25
1996	5 In.	Halloween Elf (Orange)	N/A	N/A	$14.50	$25
1996	5 In.	Holly Berry Angel	N/A	N/A	$21.50	$35
1996	5 In.	Leprechaun w/Pot O'Gold	N/A	1996	$21.50	$45
1996	5 In.	Old World Santa w/9 In. Wreath	N/A	N/A	$34.00	$65
1996	5 In.	Pixie Piccolo Player	N/A	1996	$29.50	$40
1996	5 In.	Red Christmas Elf	N/A	N/A	$14.50	$20
1996	5 In.	Sailor Duck	N/A	1996	$27.50	$55
1996	5 In.	Teepee	N/A	1997	$20.00	$40
1996	5 In.	White Christmas Lamb	N/A	N/A	$17.50	$35
1996	5 In.	Winter Elf	N/A	N/A	$14.50	$25
1996	5 In.	Wooly Lamb	N/A	N/A	$16.50	$35
1996	5 In.	Yellow Duck	N/A	N/A	$22.00	$25
1996	7 In.	Angel (Blonde Hair)	N/A	N/A	$23.50	$40
1996	7 In.	Angel w/Harp	N/A	N/A	$26.50	$45
1996	7 In.	Angel Mouse	N/A	N/A	$24.00	$40
1996	7 In.	Angel w/Musical Instrument	N/A	N/A	$22.00	$30
1996	7 In.	Baker Kid	N/A	1996	$31.00	$45
1996	7 In.	Banana Kid	N/A	1996	$27.50	$50
1996	7 In.	Bicyclist Boy Mouse	N/A	1996	$28.00	$40
1996	7 In.	Caroler Mouse w/Big Hat & Tree	N/A	N/A	$23.50	$35
1996	7 In.	Caroling Snowman	N/A	N/A	$29.50	$50
1996	7 In.	Chef Mouse	N/A	1996	$27.50	$60
1996	7 In.	Chef Santa	N/A	N/A	$29.50	$50
1996	7 In.	Christmas Party Girl Mouse	N/A	N/A	$19.50	$25
1996	7 In.	Country Boy Bunny	N/A	N/A	$25.00	$35
1996	7 In.	Country Girl Bunny	N/A	N/A	$23.00	$30

Year Introduced	Size (Inches)	Doll	Edition Size	Year Retired	Issue Price	Value
1996	7 In.	Country Girl Mouse	N/A	1997	$26.00	$40
1996	7 In.	Drummer Boy	N/A	1996	$28.50	$40
1996	7 In.	Easter Bunny Kid w/Basket	N/A	1996	$24.50	$55
1996	7 In.	E. P. Boy & Girl Bunny	N/A	1998	$50.00	$75
1996	7 In.	Hershey Kid	N/A	1996	$39.50	$65
1996	7 In.	Laundry Day Mouse w/Clothes Basket	2,845	1996	$26.00	$65
1996	7 In.	Letter to Santa Mouse	N/A	N/A	$23.00	$40
1996	7 In.	Little Mae Flower Logo w/Pin	N/A	1997	$29.50	$50
1996	7 In.	Making Friends Snowman	N/A	N/A	$27.50	$50
1996	7 In.	Moonbeam Santa Mobile	N/A	N/A	$45.50	$150
1996	7 In.	Mouse Kid	N/A	1996	$25.50	$45
1996	7 In.	Mouse w/Snowball	N/A	N/A	$19.50	$35
1996	7 In.	Mr. & Mrs. Santa Exchanging Gifts	N/A	N/A	$56.50	$75
1996	7 In.	Naughty Angel w/Black Eye	N/A	N/A	$27.50	$45
1996	7 In.	New Years Eve Mouse	N/A	1995	$19.50	$60
1996	7 In.	Old World Mrs. Santa	N/A	1996	$32.00	$50
1996	7 In.	Old World Santa	N/A	1996	$40.00	$50
1996	7 In.	Pilgrim Boy Mouse	N/A	N/A	$26.00	$30
1996	7 In.	Pilgrim Girl Mouse	N/A	N/A	$24.00	$30
1996	7 In.	P. J. Kid on Rocking Horse	N/A	N/A	$29.50	$55
1996	7 In.	Powder Puff Baby	N/A	1996	$21.00	$50
1996	7 In.	Santa	N/A	N/A	$21.50	$25
1996	7 In.	Santa Centerpiece	N/A	1996	$34.50	$55
1996	7 In.	Santa Hugging Reindeer	N/A	N/A	$51.00	$55
1996	7 In.	Santa Mouse in Chimney	N/A	N/A	$36.50	$50
1996	7 In.	Santa Skiing	N/A	N/A	$29.50	$45
1996	7 In.	Santa w/White Felt Moon (Has face and ears)	N/A	N/A	$45.00	$150
1996	7 In.	Shopping Mrs. Santa	N/A	N/A	$36.50	$40
1996	7 In.	Shopping Santa	N/A	N/A	$36.50	$40
1996	7 In.	Sleigh Ride Santa Couple	N/A	N/A	$83.50	$85
1996	7 In.	Snowball Fight Kid	N/A	1996	$30.50	$55
1996	7 In.	Snowman w/Pipe	N/A	N/A	$29.50	$35
1996	7 In.	Spider Kid	N/A	1996	$27.50	$50
1996	7 In.	St. Patrick's Day Boy	N/A	1997	$31.50	$60-$75
1996	7 In.	Sweetheart Boy Mouse	N/A	1996	$21.50	$65
1996	7 In.	Sweetheart Girl Mouse	N/A	1996	$21.50	$45
1996	7 In.	Trim Time Santa	N/A	N/A	$32.50	$35
1996	7 In.	Tuckered Boy Mouse	N/A	N/A	$22.50	$35
1996	7 In.	Tuckered Girl Mouse	N/A	N/A	$22.50	$35
1996	7 In.	Valentine Girl Kid w/Card	N/A	N/A	$27.50	$45
1996	7 In.	White Skating Mouse	N/A	N/A	$28.50	$50
1996	7 In.	Witch Kid	N/A	N/A	$31.50	$50
1996	7 In.	Witch Mouse	N/A	N/A	$27.50	$40
1996	8 In.	Corn Stalk w/Mini Pumpkin	N/A	1997	$11.95	$40
1996	8 In.	Crèche for Nativity	N/A	N/A	$39.50	$80
1996	8 In.	Ear of Corn	N/A	1996	$13.00	$40
1996	8 In.	Flowering Lilly Pad	N/A	1997	$10.00	$40
1996	10 In.	Baby Cakes Bear	N/A	N/A	$38.00	$60
1996	10 In.	Candy Basket Elves	N/A	1996	$41.50	$65

1993 – 12-inch P. J. Kids   P.J. Girl (left) is dressed in pajamas with white nightcap. $65. P.J. Boy (right) is dressed in red pajamas and a hood trimmed in red-and-white stripes. $65.

1993 – 18-inch Snowman with Broom. It wears a black hat with green ribbon, red scarf, black boots and green mittens. $75.

1994 – 3-inch Spring Pixie Pick elf with yellow felt wings. The doll wears a flower on its head and is unclothed. Mounted on floral wire. $45.

Year Introduced	Size (Inches)	Doll	Edition Size	Year Retired	Issue Price	Value
1996	10 In.	Candlemaker Woman	N/A	1996	$89.50	$225-$275
1996	10 In.	Caroling Boy Bear	N/A	N/A	$41.50	$65
1996	10 In.	Caroling Girl Bear	N/A	N/A	$41.50	$65
1996	10 In.	Caroling Reindeer	N/A	N/A	$24.50	$45
1996	10 In.	Country Boy & Girl Bunnies	N/A	1996	N/A	$45
1996	10 In.	Country Boy Bear w/Wheelbarrow	N/A	1996	$44.00	$75
1996	10 In.	Country Bumpkin Scarecrow	N/A	N/A	$37.50	$60
1996	10 In.	Country Girl Bear	N/A	1996	$44.00	$75
1996	10 In.	Doe	N/A	N/A	$22.50	$35
1996	10 In.	Easter Parade Boy Bear	2,234	1996	$42.00	$60
1996	10 In.	Easter Parade Girl Bear	2,699	1996	$42.00	$60
1996	10 In.	Fabulous 50's Couple w/Dome	1,500	1997	$150.00	$275
1996	10 In.	Flying Witch	N/A	N/A	$37.50	$55
1996	10 In.	Ghost of Christmas Future	N/A	1996	$30.00	$95-$100
1996	10 In.	Ghost of Christmas Past	N/A	1996	$40.00	$95-$100
1996	10 In.	Ghost of Christmas Present	N/A	1996	$55.50	$125
1996	10 In.	Golfer Woman	196	1996	$43.50	$75
1996	10 In.	Hook, Line & Santa	N/A	N/A	$45.00	$80
1996	10 In.	Indian Chief Bear w/Pin (Signed by Chuck)	200	1996	$130.00	$300
1996	10 In.	Indian Man	N/A	N/A	$43.00	$80
1996	48 In.	Tree Skirt	N/A	N/A	$32.50	$45
1996	10 In.	Indian Woman	N/A	N/A	$43.00	$80
1996	10 In.	Jester & Friend	N/A	1998	$34.00	$55
1996	10 In.	Joseph	N/A	N/A	$37.50	$115

1994 – Five Choir Boys, four Choir Girls and a Choir Boy with Black Eye. The 7-inch Choir Boy with Black Eye (back row) wears a green-and-white robe and holds sheet music on top of head. $50. The 7-inch Choir Girls have blonde hair and wear red-and-white gowns and green bow-ties. They hold sheet music. $45 each. The 7-inch Choir Boys wear green-and-white robes and hold sheet music. $50 each.

1993 – 10-inch Frog in Boat with green body. The doll wears white-and-blue pants and carries a fishing pole. A boat is also included. $65.

Year Introduced	Size (Inches)	Doll	Edition Size	Year Retired	Issue Price	Value
1996	10 In.	Leaping Frog	N/A	N/A	$18.00	$35
1996	10 In.	Mr. Farmer	N/A	1996	$35.00	$75
1996	10 In.	Lover Boy Bear	2,076	1996	$39.50	$75
1996	10 In.	Mary Holding Baby Jesus	N/A	N/A	$39.50	$150
1996	10 In.	Mr. Farmer (Signed by Chuck)	N/A	1996	$34.50	$75
1996	10 In.	Mr. Scrooge	N/A	1996	$37.50	$135
1996	10 In.	Mr. Scrooges Bed	N/A	1996	$43.50	$95
1996	10 In.	Mrs. Farmer	N/A	1996	$34.50	$75
1996	10 In.	Old Tyme Caroling Man	N/A	N/A	$39.00	$75
1996	10 In.	Old Tyme Caroling Woman	N/A	N/A	$39.00	$75
1996	10 In.	Old World Tree Top Angel	N/A	1996	$46.50	$85-$95
1996	10 In.	Pilgrim Man	N/A	N/A	$44.50	$75
1996	10 In.	Pilgrim Woman	N/A	N/A	$40.00	$75
1996	10 In.	Pumpkin Patch Elf	N/A	N/A	$23.50	$25
1996	10 In.	Puppies for Christmas Santa	N/A	N/A	$79.50	$110
1996	10 In.	Red Christmas Elf	N/A	N/A	$17.50	$25
1996	10 In.	Reindeer	N/A	N/A	$23.50	$25
1996	10 In.	Scarecrow (Country Bumpkin)	N/A	1997	$37.50	$60
1996	10 In.	Tennis Player (Woman)	N/A	1996	$45.95	$70
1996	10 In.	Tree Top Angel	N/A	N/A	$41.00	$65
1996	10 In.	Trick or Treat Elf	N/A	1997	$20.50	$40
1996	10 In.	Winter Elf	N/A	N/A	$18.00	$30
1996	10 In.	Wise Man Bearing Frankincense	N/A	N/A	$44.00	$115
1996	10 In.	Wiseman Bearing Gold	N/A	N/A	$43.50	$115
1996	10 In.	Wiseman Bearing Myrrh	N/A	N/A	$43.50	$160

1994 – 7-inch Artist Bunny with brown hair and mustache. The doll wears a large blue, green or pink pastel-colored beret, green jacket and pink bow. It holds an artist's brush and egg. This is a different doll from the 1993 version. $60.

1994 – 5-inch Leprechaun with Pot O' Gold wearing green clothing. It has an orange beard, pointed ears and holds a pot of gold. $45.

1994 – 7-inch Chef Santa wearing a white chef's hat with holly, green gloves and red-and-white clothing. It holds a pie. $50.

1994 – 7-inch Birthday Girl Mouse with white hair, pink ears and a light-brown body. It wears a yellow dress and yellow ribbon in its hair. The doll holds a white-and-yellow cake with candle. $40.

©AMD

©AMD

1994 – 5-inch Raincoat Duck with white body. The doll wears a yellow raincoat and holds black umbrella. $50.

Year Introduced	Size (Inches)	Doll	Edition Size	Year Retired	Issue Price	Value
1996	10 In.	Woman Golfer	N/A	1996	$44.00	$70
1996	10 In.	Woman Tennis Player	N/A	1996	$44.00	$70
1996	10 In.	Wandering Saint Nicholas	5,393	N/A	$49.00	$115-$125
1996	10 In.	Woodland Santa & Reindeer	N/A	1996	$65.50	$125
1996	12 In.	Brown Horse	N/A	1996	$35.50	$80
1996	12 In.	Cactus Set	N/A	N/A	$24.00	$45
1996	12 In.	Caroling Mrs. Santa	N/A	N/A	$45.50	$70
1996	12 In.	Caroling Santa	N/A	N/A	$55.50	$85
1996	12 In.	Carousel Horse Empress	N/A	1996	$68.00	$100
1996	12 In.	Carousel Horse #2 Noel	N/A	1996	$68.00	$100
1996	12 In.	Christmas Eve Mrs. Santa	N/A	N/A	$59.50	$60
1996	12 In.	Christmas Eve Santa	N/A	N/A	$59.50	$85
1996	12 In.	Drummer Boy	N/A	N/A	$44.50	$70
1996	12 In.	Mother Duck	N/A	1996	$49.50	$75
1996	12 In.	North Pole	N/A	N/A	$10.50	$20
1996	12 In.	Old World St. Nicholas	N/A	1996	$62.50	$75
1996	12 In.	Rose & Ivy Arbor	N/A	1996	$49.50	$75
1996	12 In.	Street Lamp	N/A	N/A	$13.95	$25-$35
1996	12 In.	Tommy Turkey	N/A	1996	$75.50	$135
1996	12 In.	Workshop Santa	N/A	N/A	$53.50	$55
1996	15 In.	Haunted Tree	N/A	1996	$44.50	$90
1996	17 In.	Teepee	N/A	N/A	$37.50	$65
1996	18 In.	Beary Christmas Stocking	90	1996	$77.50	$125
1996	18 In.	Chef Santa	N/A	N/A	$60.95	$135
1996	18 In.	Country Boy Bunny w/Wheelbarrow	N/A	1996	$67.50	$135
1996	18 In.	Country Girl Bunny	N/A	1996	$67.50	$125
1996	18 In.	Easter Parade Boy Bunny	N/A	N/A	$67.50	$95
1996	18 In.	Easter Parade Girl Bunny	N/A	N/A	$67.50	$95
1996	18 In.	Mr. Fur Santa on Stand	N/A	N/A	$49.50	$60
1996	18 In.	Mrs. Outdoor Santa	N/A	N/A	$52.50	$55
1996	18 In.	Mrs. Santa Hanging Cranberries & Popcorn	N/A	1996	$59.50	$135
1996	18 In.	Musical Caroling Santa	N/A	N/A	$57.50	$195
1996	18 In.	Old World Mrs. Santa w/Lamb	5,653	1996	$84.00	$150
1996	18 In.	Old World Santa	N/A	1996	$75.50	$125
1996	18 In.	Reindeer w/Christmas Saddlebags	N/A	N/A	$59.50	$95
1996	18 In.	Santa Hanging Gingerbread Ornament	N/A	1996	$76.50	$75-$125
1996	18 In.	Santa w/Gift List & Toy Bag	N/A	N/A	$53.50	$55
1996	18 In.	Snowman Puttin' on the Ritz	N/A	1996	$65.00	$110
1996	18 In.	Snowman w/Broom	N/A	N/A	$55.00	$75
1996	18 In.	Sunflower	N/A	1996	$23.50	$60
1996	18 In.	Tuckered Mrs. Santa & P. J. Kid	N/A	N/A	$92.00	$125
1996	18 In.	Tuckered Santa & P. J. Kid	N/A	N/A	$92.00	$125
1996	18 In.	Witchy Brew	N/A	N/A	$83.00	$135
1996	22 In.	Christmas Stocking	N/A	N/A	$19.50	$40
1996	22 In.	Green Christmas Elf	N/A	N/A	$39.50	$75
1996	22 In.	Red Christmas Elf	N/A	N/A	$39.50	$60
1996	24 In.	Country Cattail	N/A	1996	$29.00	$60
1996	25 In.	Sunflower	N/A	1996	$26.00	$60
1996	30 In.	Christmas Elf (Red)	N/A	N/A	$66.50	$110

Year Introduced	Size (Inches)	Doll	Edition Size	Year Retired	Issue Price	Value
1996	30 In.	Deck the Halls Santa	N/A	N/A	$169.50	$195
1996	30 In.	Mrs. Santa w/Cardholder Apron	N/A	N/A	$125.50	$130
1996	30 In.	Old World Mrs. Santa (Brown velour)	N/A	1966	$155.00	$325
1996	30 In.	Old World Santa (Brown velour)	N/A	1996	$160.00	$300
1996	30 In.	Shopping Mrs. Santa	N/A	N/A	$156.50	$175
1996	30 In.	Skeleton Kid	N/A	1996	$84.50	$250
1996	30 In.	Sunday Morning Santa	N/A	N/A	$125.00	$150
1996	36 In.	Old World Reindeer	N/A	N/A	$145.50	$350
1997	3 In.	Canoeing Indian Kids	N/A	1997	$37.50	$80
1997	3 In.	Indian Boy	N/A	1997	$20.00	$40
1997	3 In.	Indian Girl	N/A	N/A	$20.00	$40
1997	3 In.	Matchbox Mice	N/A	1997	$34.00	$50
1997	3 In.	Monk w/Cash	N/A	1997	$25.50	$40
1997	3 In.	Pilgrim Boy	N/A	1997	$23.50	$40
1997	3 In.	Pilgrim Girl	N/A	1997	$23.50	$40
1997	3 In.	Sleigh Ride Santa	N/A	1997	$22.50	$30
1997	3 In.	Sweet Surprise Mouse	N/A	1997	$22.50	$40
1997	3 In.	Witch Kid w/Broom	N/A	1995	N/A	$35
1997	4 In.	Puppy Present	N/A	1997	N/A	$35
1997	4 In.	Spot the Dalmatian	N/A	1997	$19.50	$45
1997	5 In.	Don't Open 'Til Christmas	625	1997	$38.50	$60
1997	5 In.	Frosty Elf	N/A	1997	N/A	$25
1997	5 In.	Holly Berry Angel	N/A	1997	N/A	$35
1997	5 In.	Mistletoe Angel	N/A	1997	$19.50	$30
1997	5 In.	Sleigh Ride Couple	2,500	1997	$100.00	$150
1997	5 In.	Workshop Elf	N/A	1997	N/A	$25
1997	7 In.	Baby New Year Kid	N/A	1997	N/A	$55
1997	7 In.	Bathtime for Buddy	3,500	1997	$54.50	$70
1997	7 In.	Caroling Snowman	N/A	1997	N/A	$50
1997	7 In.	Cleaning Day Mouse w/Mop & Bucket	N/A	1997	$26.50	$50
1997	7 In.	Clown Mouse	N/A	1997	N/A	$50
1997	7 In.	Fortunoff 75th Anniversary	750	1997	$35.00	$70
1997	7 In.	Hearth & Home Santa	N/A	1997	$38.50	$45
1997	7 In.	Ice Fishing Boy	N/A	1997	N/A	$60
1997	7 In.	Karate Kid	N/A	1997	$26.50	$40
1997	7 In.	Letter to Santa Mouse	N/A	1997	N/A	$40
1997	7 In.	Love Pumpkin Mouse	N/A	1998	$25.50	$50
1997	7 In.	Lucky the Leprechaun	N/A	1998	$34.50	$55
1997	7 In.	Naughty Angel	N/A	1997	$29.50	$40
1997	7 In.	Par Four Mouse	N/A	1997	$26.50	$50
1997	7 In.	Ringmaster Mouse (Signed by Chuck)	N/A	1997	$41.50	$55
1997	7 In.	Santa Mouse Centerpiece	N/A	1997	$28.50	$60
1997	7 In.	Skating Girl Mouse	N/A	1997	N/A	$50
1997	7 In.	St. Patrick's Day Girl	N/A	1997	$31.50	$75
1997	7 In.	Swashbuckler Boy	N/A	1997	$31.50	$50
1997	7 In.	Tags	N/A	1997	$41.50	$65
1997	7 In.	Tatters	N/A	1997	$41.50	$65
1997	7 In.	Tea for Two Logo w/Pin	N/A	1997	$29.50	$45
1997	7 In.	Tuckered Boy Mouse	N/A	1997	$22.50	$35
1997	7 In.	Tuckered Girl Mouse	N/A	1997	$22.50	$40

1994 – 7-inch Country Boy Bunny with Hoe. It has long pink ears and a white tail, wears a green checkered outfit and holds a hoe. $45.

1994 – 7-inch Easter Parade Boy and Girl Bunnies. Easter Bunny Boy (left) has pink ears and wears a green hat, pastel print shirt and green vest. It holds a cane. $35. The Easter Bunny Girl (right) has pink ears and wears a pink-and-blue dress. It holds a purse and flowers. $25.

1994 – 7-inch Football Mouse wearing orange shirt with "61" printed across the front and black shoes. The doll has a football helmet and football. $30.

1994 – 7-inch Groom Mouse with pink ears. The doll wears a black top hat and black-and-white outfit. $45.

Year Introduced	Size (Inches)	Doll	Edition Size	Year Retired	Issue Price	Value
1997	7 In.	Witch Kid	N/A	1997	N/A	$50
1997	7 In.	Wiz Kid	N/A	1997	$31.50	$45
1997	8 In.	Corn Stalk w/Pumpkin	N/A	N/A	$12.00	$25
1997	10 In.	Angel	N/A	1997	$44.50	$75
1997	10 In.	Blue (True) Santa	N/A	1997	$62.50	$125
1997	10 In.	Caroling Boy Bear	N/A	1997	$42	$65
1997	10 In.	Caroling Girl Bear	N/A	1997	$42	$65
1997	10 In.	Caroling Reindeer	N/A	1997	$26.95	$45
1997	10 In.	Country Bumpkin Scarecrow	N/A	1997	N/A	$60
1997	10 In.	Country Snowman (Feeding Birds w/Seed Bag)	N/A	1997	$37.50	$65
1997	10 In.	Country Snowman	N/A	1997	$37.50	$75
1997	10 In.	Crystal Angel (QVC Exclusive)	1,000	1997	$55.00	$125
1997	10 In.	E. P. Boy & Girl Bunny w/Pink Daffodils	N/A	1997	$89.50	$140
1997	10 In.	Flying Witch	N/A	1997	N/A	$55
1997	10 In.	Frosty Elf	N/A	1997	N/A	$30
1997	10 In.	Hook Line & Santa	N/A	1997	N/A	$80
1997	10 In.	Little Lord Taylor (Green)	375	1997	$65.00	$195
1997	10 In.	Little Lord Taylor (Red)	1,000	1997	$65.00	$115
1997	10 In.	Medicine Man	N/A	1997	$47.50	$100
1997	10 In.	Merry Christmas to All	750	1997	$84.50	$165
1997	10 In.	Mystical Santa	N/A	1997	N/A	$70
1997	10 In.	Old Tyme Caroling Man	N/A	1997	N/A	$85
1997	10 In.	Old Tyme Caroling Woman	N/A	1997	N/A	$85
1997	10 In.	Puppies for Christmas Santa	N/A	1997	N/A	$140
1997	10 In.	Roaring Twenties	N/A	1997	$160.00	$250
1997	10 In.	Scarecrow w/Cornucopia	N/A	1997	$49.50	$70
1997	10 In.	Strolling Bunny w/7 In. Baby	N/A	1997	$69.50	$125
1997	10 In.	Summer School Elf	N/A	1997	$22.50	$45
1997	10 In.	Trick or Treat Elf	N/A	1997	$40.00	$40
1997	10 In.	True Blue Santa w/Certificate	N/A	1997	$62.50	$110
1997	10 In.	Valentine Angel	N/A	1997	$45.00	$70
1997	12 In.	Buffalo	N/A	1998	$48.50	$75
1997	12 In.	Champagne Carousel Horse	N/A	1997	$67.50	$110
1997	12 In.	Christmas Eve Mrs. Santa	N/A	1997	$59.50	$60
1997	12 In.	Christmas Eve Santa	N/A	1997	$59.50	$85
1997	12 In.	Drummer Boy	N/A	1997	N/A	$75
1997	12 In.	Mr. & Mrs. Quack Quack (Set)	N/A	1997	$119.50	$225
1997	12 In.	Mrs. Quilting Santa	2,500	1997	N/A	N/A
1997	12 In.	1956 Ski Doll	3,500	N/A	$94.50	$100
1997	12 In.	Workshop Santa	N/A	1997	$55.00	$60
1997	14 In.	Roger's Clothing Store Man & Woman	3,500	N/A	$225.00	$225
1997	14 In.	Woman w/Red Felt Coat	3,500	N/A	$65.00	$65
1997	15 In.	Haunted House (Gray)	N/A	1997	$45.00	$90
1997	18 In.	Catch of the Day Santa	N/A	1997	$84.50	$135
1997	18 In.	Mrs. Santa w/Dove	N/A	1997	$67.50	$75
1997	18 In.	Reindeer	N/A	1997	$61.50	$85
1997	18 In.	Santa Hanging Ornament	N/A	1997	$64.50	$90
1997	18 In.	Spellbinder (Black-Sun & Wand)	N/A	1997	$89.50	$225-$325

Year Introduced	Size (Inches)	Doll	Edition Size	Year Retired	Issue Price	Value
1997	18 In.	'Tis the Night Before Christmas	3,500	1997	$95.00	$125
1997	18 In.	Tuckered Mrs. Santa & P. J. Kids	N/A	1997	$89.50	$125
1997	18 In.	Vineyard Monk	N/A	1997	$83.50	$100
1997	18 In.	Witchy Brew	N/A	1997	$83.50	$135
1997	22 In.	Christmas Elf (Green)	N/A	1997	$39.50	$75
1997	22 In.	Just A Jester	N/A	1997	$55	$80
1997	22 In.	Peek a Boo Stocking	N/A	1997	N/A	$40
1997	30 In.	Autumn Jester	N/A	1997	$99.50	$200
1997	30 In.	Christmas Elf (Red)	N/A	1997	$68.50	$110
1997	30 In.	Deck the Halls Santa	N/A	1997	$179.50	$180
1997	30 In.	Finishing Touch Santa	N/A	1997	$149.50	$150
1997	30 In.	Mrs. Last Minute Wrapping	N/A	1997	$149.50	$150
1997	30 In.	Mrs. Santa & Squeak	N/A	1997	$183.50	$200
1998	3 In.	Hugs & Kisses (National Open House)	N/A	1998	$24.50	$35
1998	3 In.	Little Nibbles	3,500	N/A	$40.00	$60
1998	3 In.	Sleigh Ride Santa	N/A	N/A	$23.00	$30
1998	5 In.	Christmas Monkey	N/A	1998	$22.50	$45
1998	7 In.	Barrows of Spring Wishes	1,000	1998	$29.50	$75
1998	7 In.	Blossom Mouse	N/A	1998	$28.50	$50
1998	7 In.	Clown Mouse	N/A	1998	$31.00	$50
1998	7 In.	15th Anniversary Logo Kid w/Pin	N/A	1999	$37.95	$45
1998	7 In.	Mummy Kid	N/A	1998	$32.00	$50
1998	7 In.	Paddy O'Mouse	N/A	1998	$28.00	$50
1998	7 In.	Scarecrow Kid	N/A	1998	$34.00	$50
1998	7 In.	Sports Enthusiast	3,500	N/A	$55.00	$75
1998	7 In.	Star Spangled Mouse	N/A	1998	$24.50	$75
1998	10 In.	Baking Friends	N/A	1998	$20.00	$45
1998	10 In.	Christmas Tree-ditions	1,500	1998	$94.50	$125
1998	10 In.	Fabulous Floozy Frogs (Trunk Show)	N/A	1998	$49.50	$65
1998	10 In.	Gay Nineties Couple w/Dome	N/A	1999	$174.50	$250
1998	10 In.	Harvest Angel	5,000	1998	$59.50	$80
1998	10 In.	I'm All Heart Elf	N/A	1998	$33.50	$60
1998	10 In.	Little Lord Taylor Katie Kat (w/out Signature)	250	1998	$44.50	$225
1998	10 In.	Little Lord Taylor Katie Kat (Signed by Chuck & Karen)	250	1998	$44.50	$300
1998	10 In.	Little Miss Taylor	1,300	1998	$64.50	$125
1998	10 In.	Mail Man Elf	N/A	1998	$25.00	$50
1998	10 In.	Percy the Pirate	N/A	N/A	N/A	$65
1998	10 In.	Scarecrow w/Cornucopia	N/A	1997	$44.50	$65
1998	10 In.	Sweetheart Boy Elf	N/A	1998	$20.50	$45
1998	10 In.	Sweetheart Girl Elf	N/A	1998	$20.50	$45
1998	10 In.	Tea Tyme Toads	N/A	1998	$59.50	$85
1998	10 In.	Victor Bunny	3,500	N/A	$55.00	$80
1998	10 In.	Victoria Bunny	3,500	N/A	$55.00	$80
1998	10 In.	Wanda the Witch	5,000	1998	$55.00	$75
1998	12 In.	In From the Cold	2,200	1998	$70.00	$125
1999	3 In.	Baby Jesus	N/A	N/A	$18.00	$40
1999	3 In.	Bunny	N/A	N/A	$15.00	$15

1994 – 7-inch Hershey Kid with brown hair and brown body. The doll is dressed in a silver costume to look like a Hershey's kiss. It has white sneakers and holds a Hershey's Kiss. It stands on a beige base with the Hershey's™ logo. $65.

1994 – 7-inch Hot Shot Business Girl with white hair. It wears a gray hat, burgundy coat. The doll carries a newspaper, glasses and briefcase. $50 ($450 for an example signed by Annalee and sold at auction).

1994 – 7-inch Indian Girl with black braids and a brown body. It wears a red dress trimmed in white, white head band and a red feather in her hair. It has brown moccasins and stands on a brown base. $45.

Year Introduced	Size (Inches)	Doll	Edition Size	Year Retired	Issue Price	Value
1999	3 In.	Pick of the Patch Mouse (National Open House)	N/A	1999	$24.50	$35
1999	3 In.	Surprise Birthday Bear	N/A	N/A	$19.00	$20
1999	3 In.	Sweet Pea Mouse	N/A	N/A	$25.00	$35
1999	5 In.	Nativity Angel	N/A	N/A	$20.00	$25
1999	7 In.	Après Ski	N/A	N/A	$40.00	$40
1999	7 In.	Celebrate 2000 Mouse (Signed by Chuck)	N/A	1999	$30.00	$65
1999	7 In.	Chantel's Easter Basket	42	1999	$74.50	$375
1999	7 In.	King of Hearts	43	1999	$79.50	$325
1999	7 In.	Lucky the Leprechaun	N/A	N/A	$36.00	$55
1999	7 In.	Mending My Teddy Logo w/Pin	N/A	N/A	$37.95	$40
1999	7 In.	Millennium Mouse in Ice Bucket	N/A	N/A	$35.00	$35
1999	7 In.	Nativity Drummer Boy	N/A	N/A	$30.00	$55
1999	7 In.	Rosie Girl	N/A	N/A	$39.50	$40
1999	7 In.	Spanish Couple	N/A	N/A	$95.00	$150
1999	7 In.	Summer Solitude	N/A	N/A	$39.50	$40
1999	7 In.	Teachers Pet	N/A	N/A	$40.00	$40
1999	8 In.	Dapple Grey Horse	34	1999	$29.50	$325
1999	8 In.	Donkey (Grey)	N/A	N/A	$33.00	$80
1999	8 In.	Fishin' Fun Walrus w/Fishing Pole & Fish	N/A	N/A	$40.00	$60
1999	8 in.	Gigi Poodle Lord Taylor (Signed Chuck & Karen)	350	N/A	$45.00	$175
1999	8 In.	Nautical Bear	N/A	1999	$29.50	$75
1999	8 In.	Rosemont Bear	149	1999	$36.50	$300
1999	10 In.	Christmas Cookie Boy & Girl (set)	N/A	N/A	$35.00	$90
1999	10 In.	Filene's Irish Santa	850	N/A	$60.00	$95
1999	10 In.	Floating Flo Frog (2 pc. Suit)	45	1999	$28.00	$275
1999	10 In.	Girl in Boat	200	N/A	$75.00	$175

1994 – 7-inch Indian Boy with black hair and brown body. It wears a brown vest, tan pants, a white head band, and a red feather in its hair. It has brown moccasins and carries a bow and arrows. $50.

1994 – 5-inch White Christmas Lamb (right) wearing a red Christmas hat with holly, red bow and a bell. $35. 5-inch Black Christmas Lamb wearing a red Christmas hat with holly, red bow and a bell. $35.

Year Introduced	Size (Inches)	Doll	Edition Size	Year Retired	Issue Price	Value
1999	10 In.	Hippie Couple w/Dome	N/A	1999	$195.00	$295
1999	10 In.	Holiday Best Mrs. Santa	N/A	N/A	$45.00	$55
1999	10 In.	Holiday Best Santa	N/A	N/A	$45.00	$55
1999	10 In.	Indian Chief White Eagle	N/A	N/A	$45.00	$65
1999	10 In.	Lucky Leaper Vest w/Chain	45	1999	$24.00	$225
1999	10 In.	Macys Elf	2,000	1999	$38.00	$40
1999	10 In.	Maiden Desert Bloom	N/A	N/A	$45.00	$65
1999	10 In.	Murray Chrismoose	N/A	N/A	$50.00	$105
1999	10 In.	Ox	N/A	N/A	$37.00	$85
1999	10 In.	Parker West Mouse	31	N/A	$45.00	$275
1999	10 In.	Patriotic Elf	425	N/A	$30.00	$60
1999	10 In.	Patriotic Elf Smithsonian Folk Life Festival	1,736	N/A	$59.50	$60
1999	10 In.	Peasant	N/A	N/A	$45.00	$85
1999	10 In.	Rosemary Garden Angel	27	N/A	$50.00	$150
1999	10 In.	Southern Belle	N/A	N/A	$45.00	$150
1999	10 In.	Sweetheart Elf	N/A	N/A	$21.00	$35
1999	10 In.	Sweetheart Panda	47	1999	$71.50	$325
1999	10 In.	Waldo's First Christmas	N/A	N/A	$25.00	$35
1999	10 In.	Wiseman w/Frankincense (red outfit)	N/A	N/A	$45.00	$85
1999	10 In.	Wiseman w/Gold	N/A	N/A	$45.00	$85
1999	10 In.	Wiseman w/Myrrh	N/A	N/A	$45.00	$85
1999	12 In.	Benny Bunny	N/A	N/A	$52.00	$52
1999	12 In.	Benny Bunny w/Green Watering Can	N/A	1999	$52.00	$70
1999	12 In.	Camel	N/A	N/A	$42.00	$135
1999	14 In.	Macy's 2000 Frosty Elf	2000	N/A	$38.00	$63
1999	15 In.	Painter on Scaffold	N/A	N/A	$80.00	$125
1999	18 In.	Feeding Time Mrs. Santa	37	1999	$150.00	$335
1999	18 In.	Metallic Egg Bunny	48	1999	$75.00	$250
1999	18 In.	Nautical Bunny	99	1999	$75.00	$275

1994 – 7-inch Pilgrim Girl with Pie wearing a blue checkered dress with white collar, white hat and black shoes. It holds a pie. $65.

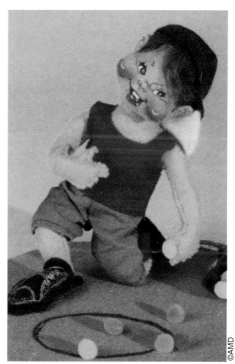

1994 – 7-inch Marble Kid with brown hair. The doll wears a red pullover tee shirt, blue jeans and black shoes. It sits on a base with game of marbles. $30.

1994 – 7-inch Pilgrim Mice Set with Basket. The Boy and Girl Mouse each have pink ears. Both are wearing blue outfits. The Boy Mouse wears a blue top hat and black belt. $75.

1994 – 7-inch Mrs. Santa with Poinsettia wearing a red-and-white poinsettia print dress, white apron and white hat with holly. It holds a poinsettia plant. $35.

1994 – 7-inch Sweetheart Boy Mouse with brown body, pink ears, long tail and painted face. It wears a black bowtie, red vest and white lace shirt. It holds a Valentine heart. $30.

1994 – 7-inch Mouse in Cornucopia with gray body and pink ears. The doll wears a blue hat and sits inside a cornucopia. $45.

1994 – 7-inch Sweetheart Girl Mouse with brown body, pink ears and blonde hair. It wears a white dress with red hearts and has a red bow in its hair. The doll holds a Valentine heart. $55.

1994 – 7-inch Snowwoman (left) wearing a red coat with white fur trim. $50. 1994 – 7-inch Ritz Snowman (right) wearing a black hat, red, green-and-white outfit, green gloves and black spats. It holds a cane. $50.

1994 – 7-inch St. Patrick Day Mouse with gray body. The doll wears a green hat and green checkered vest. $35.

105

1994 – 7-inch Thanksgiving Boy with brown hair. It wears a white bib and green pants. The doll sits on a chair holding a fork and turkey drumstick. $65.

1994 – 7-inch Yellow Flower Kid with blonde hair. The doll wears a yellow, green and purple outfit and stands on a green base. $50.

1994 – 10-inch Baseball Catcher wearing a blue-and-white uniform, striped shirt, mask and chest protector. It has blue shoes and holds a catcher's mitt. $75.

1994 – 10-inch Skier Doll, created for Christa McAuliffe annual fundraiser, wearing a black graduation hat with yellow tassel. Number 1 doll has "Annalee" printed on a white-and-blue shirt. It also wears a green jacket and black pants. The doll holds its skis and an award. $100.

1994 – 10-inch Redcoat with Cannon dressed in redcoat uniform, light tan pants and vest. It has a black tricorne hat, black shoes and comes with a cannon. $250 (signed by Annalee).

1994 – 12-inch Boy Pilgrim with Basket wearing a blue outfit with white collar and cuffs, and a blue hat with black trim. It holds a basket of vegetables. $65.

1994 – 12-inch Chef Santa with white hair and white beard. It wears a white chef's hat, white apron, green gloves and red pants. The doll holds a pie. $75.

1994 – 12-inch Mrs. Santa Cardholder wearing a poinsettia print dress, white hat, glasses and white apron. It has red leggings and black shoes. $65.

1994 – 18-inch Reindeer with Saddlebags. It is tan with white ears. $85.

1994 – 18-inch Mrs. Santa with Poinsettia, wearing a poinsettia print dress, red leggings, black slippers, white apron and white nightcap. It holds a poinsettia plant. $70.

1994 – 12-inch Santa in Chimney wearing a red Santa suit and green gloves. It holds a green bag filled with toys. $75.

1994 – 30-inch Outdoor Santa with Toy Bag wearing red-and-white Santa suit, black boots and green gloves. It carries a green bag filled with toys. $130.

1994 – 36-inch Reindeer with Saddlebags. The doll has a brown body and black nose, and carries gifts. $295.

1994 – 18-inch Easter Parade Girl Bunny with Basket. It has pink ears and wears a pastel print hat and Easter outfit. It has pink shoes, a pink purse, and holds flowers in hand. $85.

1994 – 18-inch Country Girl Bunny with basket (left) and Country Boy Bunny with hoe (right). Both have pink ears and wear green checkered outfits. $95 each.

1996 – 5-inch Pixie Piccolo Player wearing a royal-blue hat and coat, white lace shirt and light-blue pants. The doll has brown boots and plays a piccolo. $40.

1995 – 3-inch Wynken, Blynken, and Nod, sitting in a boat, dressed like pirates. The boat has a patched red-and-white striped sail. $100.

1994 – 18-inch Witch with white hair and painted face. It wears a black hat and black cape and red-and-white striped pants, and holds a broom. $95.

1995 – 7-inch Nashville Boy wearing a black cowboy hat, red shirt with hearts and white pull string, blue jeans and black boots. It is playing a fiddle. $60.

1995 – 7-inch Nashville Girl wearing a black cowboy hat, white blouse, red dress with hearts and white lace trim and black boots. $60.

1995 – 7-inch Pilgrim Boy with Fawn. The boy wears a blue suit and hat, white collar, white sleeves and black belt. It is hugging a 5-inch fawn. $65.

112

©AMD

1995 – 10-inch Canadian Mountie with Horse. The doll sits on a horse and wears a Mountie's hat and uniform. It holds a red-and-white Canadian flag. $275.

©AMD

1995 – 10-inch Canadian Mountie wearing Mountie's hat and uniform (red jacket, black pants). The doll holds a red-and-white Canadian flag. $150.

©AMD

1996 – 3-inch Canoeing Indian Kids. They are Boy and Girl Indian Kids sitting in a canoe. $60.

113

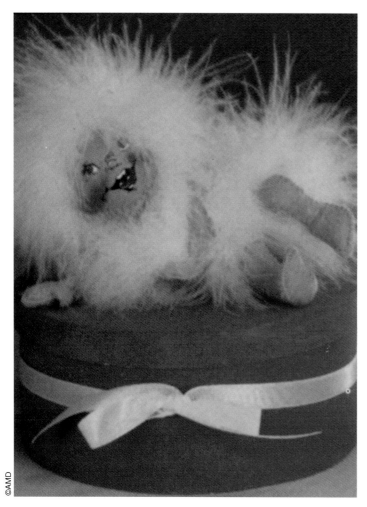

©AMD

©AMD

1996 – 7-inch Powder Puff Baby dressed in white fur. The doll sits on a round pink powder puff box. $50.

1996 – 10-inch Hook, Line and Santa. Santa wears a tan hat, tan vest, red shirt and brown pants. He has green boots and holds a fishing rod and creel with fish. $80 (signed and numbered with a brass plaque).

1996 – 7-inch Easter Parade Girl and Boy Bunny. The Girl Bunny (left) wears a white hat and pastel striped dress. It holds flowers. $45. The Boy Bunny (right) has white hair and wears a pastel striped vest, blue bow tie and white top hat with blue ribbon trim. It carries a cane. $45.

©AMD

114

1997 – 7-inch Wiz Kid wearing a red cone hat, red gown with gold stars and black shoes. The doll holds a wand with star and a trick-or-treat bag. $45.

1997 – 7-inch Lucky the Leprechaun with long orange beard. It wears green clothing, black shoes and a brown hat. The doll holds a pipe in hand. There are two mushrooms on base, begorrah, with garland of shamrocks in a circle. $55.

1997 – 7-inch Ice Fishing Boy wearing a beige hat, green shirt, brown pants and black boots. It has a brown scarf and red gloves, and sits on a galvanized fishing bucket. A fish is visible in the snow on the base. $60.

1997 – 10-inch Little Lord Taylor in a forest-green outfit. This doll was sold exclusively in Lord and Taylor Stores. $195.

1997 – 7-inch Karate Kid with brown hair. The doll wears a white karate suit trimmed in red. A gold karate metal is wrapped around its neck. $40.

1997 – 10-inch Old Tyme Caroling Man wearing a black hat, brown fur coat, black robe and boots. It holds Christmas carol sheet music. $85.

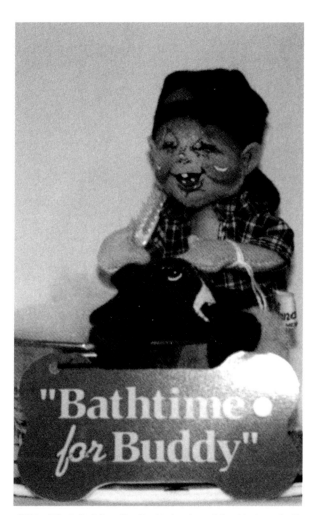

1997 – 7-inch Bathtime For Buddy is a boy giving his dog a bath in galvanized tub. $70.

1997 – 7-inch Swashbuckler Boy with black pirate hat, red bandanna, red-and-white striped shirt and black pants. It has a gold earring in one ear and holds a sword and a trick-or-treat bag. $50.

1997 – 10-inch Old Tyme Caroling Woman with white hair. She wears a blue-and-green velour hat and coat, white dress and green gloves. The doll holds Christmas carol sheet music. $85.

117

1997 – 18-inch Catch of the Day Santa with white beard and red body. It wears a green-and-black checkered shirt, tan vest and hat and brown boots. It holds a fishing pole, and a frog has found its way into the vest pocket. $135.

1997 – 12-inch Drummer Boy wearing a black hat, blue checkered scarf and red jacket with two patches. It has white gloves and black shoes and plays a drum. $75.

1997 – Man and Woman (reproductions shown here) were made for Roger's Clothing Store. The Man is 15-5/8 inches high with a 5½-inch base diameter; The original wore a black hat, blue suit, white shirt, black shoes. The Woman measures 14-3/8 inches high with a 4 ½-inch base diameter; The original had blonde hair, white hat, pink dress with white gloves, white shoes. $225 for the pair.

118

1997 – 30-inch Autumn Jester dressed in yellow, orange and brown outfit. $200.

1997 – 30-inch Mrs. Last Minute Wrapping with white hair. It wears a green hat and apron, red blouse, red leggings and patchwork dress. It has black shoes. $150.

1997 – 18-inch Vineyard Monk with a brown beard. It wears a maroon robe and skull cap and brown belt. It holds grapevine and has a brass key on a rope around its neck. $100.

2000+

2000 – This is a 7-inch Heartfelt Boy Mouse with black body, white face and tail, white hair and pink ears. It wears a black top hat, white lace jabot, and red bow tie. $35. 2000 – It is shown with a 7-inch Heartfelt Girl Mouse with white body and hair, and pink ears, wearing a red-and-white Valentine dress with hearts and kisses. The Girl Mouse holds a pink rose. $35.

Year Introduced	Size (Inches)	Doll	Edition Size	Year Retired	Issue Price	Value
2000	3 In.	Sunshine Pin	N/A	N/A	$6.00	$6
2000	3 In.	"Waiting on Christmas" Elf	N/A	N/A	$20.00	$38
2000	3 In.	White Bunny	N/A	N/A	$15.00	$30
2000	4 In.	Playful Pup	N/A	N/A	$18.00	$30
2000	4 In.	Santa Claus Cat	N/A	N/A	$21.00	$32
2000	5 In.	Christmas Elf (Red)	N/A	N/A	$16.00	$17
2000	5 In.	Christmas Elf (White)	N/A	N/A	$16.00	$25
2000	5 In.	Cupid	N/A	N/A	$23.50	$35
2000	5 In.	"Fill 'er Up" Elf	N/A	N/A	$24.00	$40
2000	5 In.	Halloween Elf (Black)	N/A	N/A	$20.00	$25
2000	5 In.	Halloween Elf (Orange)	N/A	N/A	$20.00	$25
2000	5 In.	Nativity Angel	N/A	N/A	$20.00	$25
2000	5 In.	Precious Angel Baby	N/A	N/A	$19.00	$30
2000	5 In.	Yellow Duck	N/A	N/A	$22.00	$35
2000	7 In.	"All Mine" Mouse	N/A	N/A	$27.00	$40
2000	7 In.	"Almost There" Turtle	N/A	N/A	$24.00	$35
2000	7 In.	"All Wrapped Up" Mouse	N/A	N/A	$27.00	$40
2000	7 In.	Angel's First Wings	N/A	N/A	$26.00	$35
2000	7 In.	Angel Mouse	N/A	N/A	$26.00	$40
2000	7 In.	"Armed & Ready" Mouse	N/A	N/A	$27.00	$40
2000	7 In.	Autumn Palette Mouse	N/A	N/A	$32.00	$48
2000	7 In.	Baby Boy Mouse	N/A	N/A	$25.00	$40
2000	7 In.	Baby Girl Mouse	N/A	N/A	$25.00	$40
2000	7 In.	Ballerina Mouse	N/A	N/A	$26.00	$40
2000	7 In.	Bat Kid	N/A	N/A	$30.00	$40
2000	7 In.	Beekeeper Mouse	N/A	N/A	$28.00	$42
2000	7 In.	Beth's Bubble	N/A	N/A	$34.00	$45
2000	7 In.	Bingo Mouse	N/A	N/A	$28.00	$40
2000	7 In.	Bride Mouse	N/A	N/A	$25.00	$30
2000	7 In.	Bride & Groom	N/A	N/A	$75.00	$100
2000	7 In.	Buck-a-Roo Mouse	N/A	N/A	$28.00	$40
2000	7 In.	Bumblebee Kid	N/A	N/A	$30.00	$40
2000	7 In.	Bunny w/Butterfly	N/A	N/A	$22.00	$40
2000	7 In.	Candy Cane Mouse	N/A	N/A	$27.00	$40
2000	7 In.	Catching Snowflakes	N/A	N/A	$25.00	$40
2000	7 In.	Chef Santa	N/A	N/A	$35.00	$50
2000	7 In.	Chores First Collector Kid	N/A	N/A	$40.00	$40
2000	7 In.	Christmas Booty Mouse	N/A	N/A	$27.00	$40
2000	7 In.	Christmas Scents Skunk	N/A	N/A	$26.00	$38
2000	7 In.	Christmas Tales Mouse	N/A	N/A	$27.00	$40
2000	7 In.	Christmas Tweets Santa	N/A	N/A	$32.00	$48
2000	7 In.	Church Mouse	N/A	N/A	$29.00	$45
2000	7 In.	Colonial Boy Mouse	N/A	N/A	$28.00	$35
2000	7 In.	Colonial Girl Mouse	N/A	N/A	$28.00	$35
2000	7 In.	Cool Buddies Snowman	N/A	N/A	$36.00	$47
2000	7 In.	Count Mouse	N/A	N/A	$26.00	$30
2000	7 In.	Country Snowman	N/A	N/A	$30.00	$45
2000	7 In.	Dentist Mouse	N/A	N/A	$25.00	$50
2000	7 In.	Devil Mouse	N/A	N/A	$26.00	$35
2000	7 In.	Doctor Mouse	N/A	N/A	$25.00	$40
2000	7 In.	Dracula Kid	N/A	N/A	$30.00	$40

2000 – 3-inch Holly Elf Ornament with white hair and body. It sits on a dark-green and light-green holly leaf with red berries. The elf also has holly leaves on its head. $30.

2000 – 3-inch Penguin Ornament with yellow beak, black arms and white body. It wears a red cone hat and blue scarf, and holds a mint. $30.

** Signed by Annalee

2000 – 3-inch Snowman Ornament with white body. The ornament wears a black top hat, yellow gloves, red scarf and green ear muffs. $30.

2000 – 7-inch Midnight Snack Kid with blonde hair. The doll wears Christmas holly pajamas and holds a cookie and a glass of milk. A cat sits at the doll's feet. $35.

Year Introduced	Size (Inches)	Doll	Edition Size	Year Retired	Issue Price	Value
2000	7 In.	Dressin' Like Mommy Logo w/Pin	N/A	N/A	$40.00	$40
2000	7 In.	Egg Centric	N/A	N/A	$20.00	$38
2000	7 In.	Father Christmas Mouse	N/A	N/A	$27.00	$38
2000	7 In.	Finishing Touches Mouse	N/A	N/A	$27.00	$45
2000	7 In.	First Aid Mouse	N/A	N/A	$29.00	$45
2000	7 In.	First Class Mouse	N/A	N/A	$27.00	$45
2000	7 In.	Frankenstein Kid	N/A	N/A	$30.00	$55
2000	7 In.	Gardening Mouse	N/A	N/A	$26.00	$40
2000	7 In.	Gift Mouse	N/A	N/A	$26.00	$43
2000	7 In.	Gifts of Cheese Mouse	N/A	N/A	$27.00	$40
2000	7 In.	Good Fairy	N/A	N/A	$42.00	$55
2000	7 In.	Granny Mouse	N/A	N/A	$25.00	$40
2000	7 In.	Groom Mouse	N/A	N/A	$25.00	$30
2000	7 In.	"Hang My Stocking" Mouse	N/A	N/A	$27.00	$40
2000	7 In.	Heart Felt Boy Mouse (Black body)	N/A	N/A	$25.00	$35
2000	7 In.	Heart Felt Girl Mouse (White body)	N/A	N/A	$25.00	$35
2000	7 In.	Heavenly Treasures Angel	N/A	N/A	$35.00	$45
2000	7 In.	Hobo Mouse	N/A	N/A	$26.00	$35
2000	7 In.	Hobby Horse Rider	N/A	N/A	$34.00	$45
2000	7 In.	Holiday Lights Mouse	N/A	N/A	$25.00	$40
2000	7 In.	Irish Boy Mouse	N/A	N/A	$26.00	$50
2000	7 In.	Jeff & Jack O' Lantern	N/A	N/A	$40.00	$50
2000	7 In.	Katie O' Mouse	N/A	N/A	$24.00	$50
2000	7 In.	Kisses For Sale	N/A	N/A	$34.00	$40
2000	7 In.	Lemonade Stand	N/A	N/A	$34.00	$40
2000	7 In.	Meg Mouse	N/A	N/A	$26.00	$50
2000	7 In.	Midnight Snack Kid	N/A	N/A	$32.00	$35
2000	7 In.	Millennium Mouse	N/A	N/A	$35.00	$55
2000	7 In.	Mouse Express	N/A	N/A	$27.00	$40
2000	7 In.	Mouse in Popcorn Basket	N/A	N/A	$25.00	$40
2000	7 In.	Mr. Fix-it Mouse	N/A	N/A	$26.00	$40
2000	7 In.	Mrs. Claus Cookie Jar	N/A	N/A	$36.00	$55
2000	7 In.	Mrs. Touch of Gold	N/A	N/A	$34.00	$50
2000	7 In.	Mrs. White Christmas	N/A	N/A	$34.00	$45
2000	7 In.	Mrs. With the Wishes	N/A	N/A	$36.00	$55
2000	7 In.	Music From On High Angel	N/A	N/A	$35.00	$45
2000	7 In.	New Years Mouse	N/A	N/A	$26.00	$45
2000	7 In.	Nurse Kid	N/A	N/A	$30.00	$40
2000	7 In.	Off to Skate Girl	N/A	N/A	$30.00	$45
2000	7 In.	Patrick Mouse	N/A	N/A	$26.00	$50
2000	7 In.	Patriotic Girl #1 (Sue Coffee Exclusive)	500	2000	$45.00	$150
2000	7 In.	Patriotic Girl #2 (Sue Coffee Exclusive)	600	2000	$50.00	$50-$125
2000	7 In.	Patriotic Boy (Sue Coffee Exclusive)	1200	2000	$55.00	$55
2000	7 In.	Paula in the Leaf Pile	N/A	N/A	$40.00	$50
2000	7 In.	Pick 'N Time Boy	N/A	N/A	$40.00	$55
2000	7 In.	Quilting Mouse	N/A	N/A	$25.00	$40
2000	7 In.	Rooster Kid	N/A	N/A	$30.00	$40
2000	7 In.	Sailor Boy Mouse	N/A	N/A	$25.00	$50
2000	7 In.	Sailor Girl Mouse	N/A	N/A	$25.00	$45
2000	7 In.	Santa's Cookie Jar	N/A	N/A	$34.00	$55
2000	7 In.	Santa's Helper Mouse	N/A	N/A	$28.00	$40

Year Introduced	Size (Inches)	Doll	Edition Size	Year Retired	Issue Price	Value
2000	7 In.	Santa's Letters	N/A	N/A	$30.00	$55
2000	7 In.	Shanna's Scarecrow	N/A	N/A	$40.00	$50
2000	7 In.	Sharing the Light Mouse	N/A	N/A	$27.00	$30
2000	7 In.	Shooting Star Angel	N/A	N/A	$30.00	$40
2000	7 In.	Skeleton Mouse	N/A	N/A	$26.00	$35
2000	7 In.	Sledding Away Mouse	N/A	N/A	$27.00	$40
2000	7 In.	Slip Sliding Snowman	N/A	N/A	$30.00	$50
2000	7 In.	Snapshot Mouse	N/A	N/A	$29.00	$40
2000	7 In.	Snowman	N/A	N/A	$28.00	$35
2000	7 In.	Snowy Gentleman	N/A	N/A	$30.00	$50
2000	7 In.	Snowy Lady	N/A	N/A	$30.00	$50
2000	7 In.	Soccer Kid	N/A	N/A	$40.00	$40
2000	7 In.	Spring Boy Bunny	N/A	N/A	$27.00	$45
2000	7 In.	Spring Girl Bunny	N/A	N/A	$27.00	$45
2000	7 In.	Steve Raking Leaves	N/A	N/A	$40.00	$50
2000	7 In.	Stocking Stuffer Mouse	N/A	N/A	$29.00	$40
2000	7 In.	Stay Put Snowman	N/A	N/A	$30.00	$50
2000	7 In.	Sunny Gardener Girl	N/A	N/A	$34.00	$50
2000	7 In.	Sunday Best Boy Mouse	N/A	N/A	$25.00	$45
2000	7 In.	Sunday Best Girl Mouse	N/A	N/A	$25.00	$45
2000	7 In.	Sweet Dreams Kid	N/A	N/A	$32.00	$50
2000	7 In.	Sweet Scents Mouse	N/A	N/A	$24.00	$35
2000	7 In.	Sweetheart Boy Mouse	N/A	N/A	$25.00	$30
2000	7 In.	Sweetheart Girl Mouse	N/A	N/A	$25.00	$30
2000	7 In.	Sweet Tooth Mouse	N/A	N/A	$27.00	$40
2000	7 In.	"This Gift Stinks" Mouse	N/A	N/A	$27.00	$40
2000	7 In.	Tiger Kid	N/A	N/A	$30.00	$40
2000	7 In.	Timmy Turtle	N/A	N/A	$24.00	$30
2000	7 In.	Toasty Treats Snowman	N/A	N/A	$30.00	$50
2000	7 In.	Time For a Trim	N/A	N/A	$60.00	$75
2000	7 In.	Touch of Gold Santa	N/A	N/A	$34.00	$50
2000	7 In.	Valentine Surprise Mouse	N/A	N/A	$25.00	$45
2000	7 In.	Violet Mouse	N/A	N/A	$26.00	$40
2000	7 In.	White Christmas Santa	N/A	N/A	$36.00	$45
2000	7 In.	With Love From Above Angel	N/A	N/A	$35.00	$45
2000	7 In.	Who's Next Mouse	N/A	N/A	$27.00	$40
2000	7 In.	Xmas Best Girl	N/A	N/A	$40.00	$50
2000	8 In.	Batty for Treats Bear	N/A	N/A	$29.00	$40
2000	8 In.	Bear-ly Awake	N/A	N/A	$30.00	$45
2000	8 In.	Bear-ly Flying	N/A	N/A	$29.00	$45
2000	8 In.	Bearing Down	N/A	N/A	$30.00	$45
2000	8 In.	Bear-ly Fits	N/A	N/A	$32.00	$48
2000	8 In.	Bear-ly Skating	N/A	N/A	$30.00	$50
2000	8 In.	Bearing Greetings	N/A	N/A	$25.00	$42
2000	8 In.	Bristo Bear	N/A	N/A	$36.00	$55
2000	8 In.	Catch a Star Bear	N/A	N/A	$30.00	$45
2000	8 In.	Cele-bear-tion	N/A	N/A	$30.00	$50
2000	8 In.	Christmas Morning Bear	N/A	N/A	$30.00	$45
2000	8 In.	Country Crow	N/A	N/A	$54.00	$54
2000	8 In.	Darla	N/A	N/A	$36.00	$40
2000	8 In.	Fishing Bear	N/A	N/A	$36.00	$53

2000 – 7-inch Patriotic Boy, a Sue Coffee Exclusive. It wears a red-and-white striped stovepipe hat with blue rim, red-and-white striped pants and blue shoes. It has a blue bow and comes with removable firecracker. The doll stands on a beige base. Original retail price $55.

2000 – 7-inch Patriotic Girl #1, a Sue Coffee Exclusive. It wears a white straw hat, red-and-white striped sun dress with red collar. It has red shoes and a blue bow and comes with removable flag and stand. It stands on a beige base. $150.

2000 – 7-inch Patriotic Girl #2, a Sue Coffee Exclusive. It wears a white sailor hat with a blue "A" and a red-and-white striped middy-style dress with blue collar. It has blue shoes and a red bow. The doll comes with removable flag and stand, and stands on a beige base. $125.

2000 – 7-inch Sharing the Light Mouse with white body and tail, and pink ears. The doll wears a green top hat and multi-colored scarf. It holds a Christmas card and lantern. $30.

Year Introduced	Size (Inches)	Doll	Edition Size	Year Retired	Issue Price	Value
2000	8 In.	Foliage Frolic Bear	N/A	N/A	$32.00	$50
2000	8 In.	Formal Delivery Penguin	N/A	N/A	$24.00	$35
2000	8 In.	Gift List Bear	N/A	N/A	$30.00	$45
2000	8 In.	Grandma Bear	N/A	N/A	$30.00	$45
2000	8 In.	Grandpa Bear	N/A	N/A	$30.00	$45
2000	8 In.	Harvest Boy Bear	N/A	N/A	$33.00	$53
2000	8 In.	Harvest Girl Bear	N/A	N/A	$33.00	$53
2000	8 In.	Honey Bee Bear	N/A	N/A	$26.00	$30
2000	8 In.	Horsing Around Bear	N/A	N/A	$30.00	$45
2000	8 In.	'Lil Devil Bear	N/A	N/A	$28.00	$40
2000	8 In.	Native Boy Bear	N/A	N/A	$33.00	$53
2000	8 In.	Native Girl Bear	N/A	N/A	$33.00	$53
2000	8 In.	Out Foxed	N/A	N/A	$34.00	$45
2000	8 In.	Patriotic Bear	N/A	N/A	$36.00	$60
2000	8 In.	Scarecrow Bear	N/A	N/A	$36.00	$48
2000	8 In.	Secret Santa Bear	N/A	N/A	$30.00	$45
2000	8 In.	Stardurst Angel Bear	N/A	N/A	$30.00	$45
2000	8 In.	Startled Bear	N/A	N/A	$30.00	$45
2000	8 In.	Tina Ballerina Elephant	N/A	N/A	$33.00	$38
2000	8 In.	Too-Too Clean Hippo	N/A	N/A	$30.00	$40
2000	8 In.	Toy Bag Bear	N/A	N/A	$30.00	$45
2000	8 In.	Tu-Tu Cute Hippo	N/A	N/A	$39.50	$50
2000	8 In.	Viola in Her Valentine	N/A	N/A	$28.00	$45
2000	8 In.	Witch Bear	N/A	N/A	$29.00	$35
2000	10 In.	Brightly Bones Elf	N/A	N/A	$24.00	$43
2000	10 In.	Candlelight Stories Elf	N/A	N/A	$30.00	$40
2000	10 In.	Christmas Elf (Red)	N/A	N/A	$20.00	$25
2000	10 In.	Christmas Lights Elf	N/A	N/A	$22.00	$40
2000	10 In.	Cookie Cook Gingerbread Boy	N/A	N/A	$36.00	$60
2000	10 In.	Cookie Cook Gingerbread Girl	N/A	N/A	$36.00	$60
2000	10 In.	Elfin Delivery	N/A	N/A	$30.00	$45
2000	10 In.	Elf Helper	N/A	N/A	$24.00	$35
2000	10 In.	Elf & Purr-fect Pals	N/A	N/A	$24.00	$45
2000	10 In.	Elf Treats	N/A	N/A	$22.00	$22
2000	10 In.	Fishin' Freddie Frog	N/A	N/A	$26.00	$45
2000	10 In.	Flappin' Fran Flamingo	N/A	N/A	$35.00	$45
2000	10 In.	Floatin' Flo Frog	N/A	N/A	$28.00	$40
2000	10 In.	Frosty Elf	N/A	N/A	$22.00	$22
2000	10 In.	Heavenly Presence	N/A	N/A	$42.00	$50
2000	10 In.	Holiday Fun Deer	N/A	N/A	$28.00	$42
2000	10 In.	Holiday Gift Mouse	N/A	N/A	$45.00	$50
2000	10 In.	Irish Lamb	N/A	N/A	$30.00	$55
2000	10 In.	Jest for Baby	N/A	N/A	$30.00	$40
2000	10 In.	Leprechaun (holds mug of beer)	N/A	N/A	$24.00	$50
2000	10 In.	Lucky Leaper	N/A	N/A	$24.00	$45
2000	10 In.	Misspelled Frog	N/A	N/A	$25.00	$40
2000	10 In.	Mother-To-Be Mouse	N/A	N/A	$40.00	$55
2000	10 In.	Playful Kitty	N/A	N/A	$32.00	$45
2000	10 In.	Purr-fectly Warm Kitty	N/A	N/A	$43.00	$65
2000	10 In.	Rosemary Gardener	N/A	N/A	$40.00	$50
2000	10 In.	Sammy Snail	N/A	N/A	$27.00	$30

Year Introduced	Size (Inches)	Doll	Edition Size	Year Retired	Issue Price	Value
2000	10 In.	Scuba Frog	N/A	N/A	$30.00	$45
2000	10 In.	Stocking Stuffer Elf	N/A	N/A	$30.00	$45
2000	10 In.	Taking a Break Elf	N/A	N/A	$26.00	$42
2000	10 In.	Toil 'n Trouble Witch	N/A	N/A	$58.00	$70
2000	10 In.	Toni Toad	N/A	N/A	$24.00	$45
2000	10 In.	Whitetail Buck	N/A	N/A	$24.00	$35
2000	12 In.	Benny Bunny	N/A	N/A	$50.00	$50
2000	12 In.	Bunny Kid	N/A	N/A	$40.00	$60
2000	12 In.	Clown	N/A	N/A	$60.00	$70
2000	12 In.	Hanna Holstein	N/A	N/A	$50.00	$65
2000	12 In.	Howie Holstein	N/A	N/A	$50.00	$65
2000	12 In.	Making Friends Bunny	N/A	N/A	$44.00	$65
2000	12 In.	Mrs. Gift of Gold	N/A	N/A	$56.00	$85
2000	12 In.	Mrs. Touch of Gold	N/A	N/A	$56.00	$85
2000	12 In.	Sailor Boy Bunny	N/A	N/A	$50.00	$85
2000	12 In.	Sailor Girl Bunny	N/A	N/A	$50.00	$75
2000	12 In.	Sherlock Hare	N/A	N/A	$44.00	$65
2000	12 In.	Snowy Reindeer	N/A	N/A	$44.00	$80
2000	12 In.	Star Bright Angel	N/A	N/A	$42.00	$50
2000	12 In.	Touch of Gold Santa	N/A	N/A	$56.00	$85
2000	12 In.	Whitetail Deer	N/A	N/A	$45.00	$68
2000	12 In.	Wrapping Gold Santa	N/A	N/A	$56.00	$85
2000	13 In.	Heather's Heart	N/A	N/A	$60.00	$75
2000	13 In.	Jack	N/A	N/A	$50.00	$75
2000	13 In.	Jill	N/A	N/A	$50.00	$75
2000	13 In.	Lovable Larry	N/A	N/A	$50.00	$75
2000	13 In.	Marvin the Magician	N/A	N/A	$60.00	$80
2000	13 In.	Santa's New Boots	N/A	N/A	$50.00	$60
2000	13 In.	Santa w/ Sack of Gifts	N/A	N/A	$50.00	$75
2000	13 In.	White Christmas Santa	N/A	N/A	$50.00	$75
2000	14 In.	Frosty Elf	N/A	N/A	$30.00	$30
2000	18 In.	Cheer Up Baby	N/A	N/A	$70.00	$80
2000	18 In.	Christmas Cheer (Mrs.)	N/A	N/A	$70.00	$110
2000	18 In.	Christmas Cheer Santa	N/A	N/A	$70.00	$110
2000	18 In.	Dress For You Snowman	N/A	N/A	$54.00	$75
2000	18 In.	Dress For You Snowwoman	N/A	N/A	$54.00	$75
2000	18 In.	Just in Time Bunny	N/A	N/A	$60.00	$85
2000	18 In.	Mrs. Claus w/Muff	N/A	N/A	$70.00	$95
2000	18 In.	Mrs. White Christmas	N/A	N/A	$70.00	$95
2000	18 In.	Off To Bed Baby	N/A	N/A	$50.00	$85
2000	18 In.	Patchwork Bunny	N/A	N/A	$50.00	$75
2000	18 In.	Santa w/ Present	N/A	N/A	$70.00	$95
2000	18 In.	Spring Boy Bunny	N/A	N/A	$65.00	$75
2000	18 In.	Spring Girl Bunny	N/A	N/A	$65.00	$75
2000	18 In.	Sunday Best Boy Bunny	N/A	N/A	$65.00	$75
2000	18 In.	Sunday Best Girl Bunny	N/A	N/A	$65.00	$75
2000	18 In.	White Christmas Santa	N/A	N/A	$70.00	$125
2000	22 In.	Frosty Elf	N/A	N/A	$39.50	$60
2000	22 In.	Peek-a-boo Stocking	N/A	N/A	$24.00	$35
2000	30 In.	Caroler Man	N/A	N/A	$160.00	$200-295
2000	30 In.	Caroler Woman	N/A	N/A	$160.00	$200-250

2000 – 7-inch Sunday Best Girl Mouse (left) with white body. It wears a white lace hat with pink trim and navy-blue floral outfit. It holds flowers. $30. 2000 – 7-inch Sunday Best Boy Mouse (right) with white body. It wears a white hat with pink trim, navy-blue floral outfit and a pink bow tie. $30.

2000 – 8-inch Baker Mouse Ornament with a brown body. It wears a red chef's hat and sits on white cookie dough holding a rolling pin. $30.

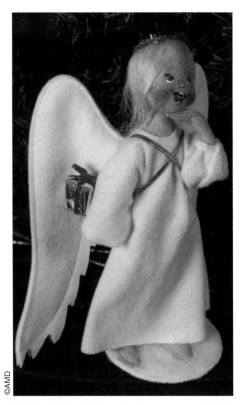

Year Introduced	Size (Inches)	Doll	Edition Size	Year Retired	Issue Price	Value
2000	30 In.	Mrs. Snack Time	N/A	N/A	$140.00	$160
2000	30 In.	Sailor Boy Bunny	N/A	N/A	$145.00	$195-225
2000	30 In.	Scarecrow	N/A	N/A	$100.00	$125-$150
2000	30 In.	Snack Time Santa	N/A	N/A	$140.00	$150
2000	30 In.	Traditional Santa	N/A	N/A	$180.00	$200
2000	36 In.	Snowy Reindeer	N/A	N/A	$156.00	$200
2001	7 In.	Bountiful Harvest Mouse (Sponsor Store Exclusive)	N/A	2001	$38.00	$75
2001	7 In	Christmas Bells Mouse	N/A		$30.00	$50
2001	7 In	Christmas Candy Mouse	N/A	2001	$27.00	$55
2001	7 In.	Firecracker Mouse	N/A	2001	$25.00	$40
2001	7 In	Firefighter Mouse	N/A	2001	$26.00	$50
2001	7 In	Let's Build A Snowman	N/A	2001	$27.00	$50
2001	7 In.	Old Glory Mouse	N/A	2001	$26.00	$50
2001	7 In.	Pilgrim Boy Mouse	N/A	2001	$28.00	$55
2001	7 In.	Pilgrim Girl Mouse	N/A	2001	$28.00	$55
2001	7 In	Sailor Boy Mouse	N/A	2001	$25.00	$50
2001	7 In.	Sailor Girl Mouse	N/A	2001	$25.00	$45
2001	7 In.	Witchy Mouse	N/A	2001	$26.00	$50
2001	7 In	Yuletide Mouse	N/A	2001	$25.00	$50

2000 – 10-inch Heavenly Presence angel with blonde hair and white wings. The doll wears a long white dress and gold halo. It holds a Christmas gift behind its back and stands on a white base. $50.

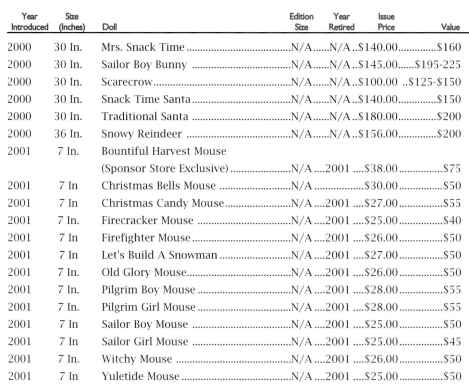

2000 – 7-inch Sweetheart Boy Mouse (left) with brown hair and body, and pink ears. It wears a red-and-white vest and white lace jabot. $30. 2000 – 7-inch Sweetheart Girl Mouse (right) with white hair and body, and pink ears. It wears a red-and-white dress with white lace trim. $30.

2000 – 12-inch Benny Bunny with tan body and pink ears. It wears blue overalls, green hat and a green-and-white checkered shirt. The doll holds a water can, which was available first in galvanized metal, then in green. $50.

Year Introduced	Size (Inches)	Doll	Edition Size	Year Retired	Issue Price	Value
2001	8 In	First Mate Bear	N/A	2001	$30.00	$55
2001	10 In.	Wizard (Sponsor Store Exclusive)	N/A	2001	$40.50	$75
2001	10 In.	Patriotic Clown (Sue Coffee Exclusive)	1000	2001	$45.00	$45
2001	10 In.	Gifts For All Man	N/A	2001	$45.00	$70
2001	10 In.	Gifts For All Woman	N/A	2001	$45.00	$70
2001	10 In	Wispy Witch	N/A	2001	$34.50	$60
2001	10 In	Witchy's Wild Ride	N/A	2001	$39.00	$65
2001	13 In.	Pilgrim Man	N/A	2001	$50.00	$85
2001	13 In.	Pilgrim Woman	N/A	2001	$50.00	$85
2001	13 In	Ye Old Caroller Man	N/A	2001	$52.00	$75
2001	13 In	Ye Old Caroller Woman	N/A	2001	$52.00	$75
2001	15 In	Leprechaun Treasure (green coat, auburn beard)	N/A	2001	$50.00	$75

2000 – 13-inch White Christmas Santa dressed in a white coat and white boots. He holds a bag filled with gifts. $75.

2000 – 10-inch Sammy the Snail with a yellow and chartreuse shell and blue eyes. It wears a black hat. $30.

2000 – 7-inch Timmy Turtle with green body and printed shell. It wears a black hat and black bow tie. $30.

©AMD

2000 – 18-inch Mrs. Claus (left) with white hair. It wears a long teal-blue coat with white trim and a green-and-gold print scarf. It holds a muff. $95. 2000 – 18-inch Santa with Presents (right) wearing a long teal-blue coat with white trim and white boots. It holds Christmas gifts. $95.

©AMD

2000 - 18-inch Sunday Best Boy Bunny (left) with pink ears, white hair and a white furry body. It wears a navy-blue flowered vest, pink bow tie and white jabot. $75. 2000 - 18-inch Sunday Best Girl Bunny (right) with pink ears, white hair and a white furry body. It wears a navy-blue flowered dress with pearl necklace. It has a bow in its hair. $75.

2001 – 10-inch Patriotic Clown, a Sue Coffee Exclusive. It wears a red, white and blue stovepipe hat with blue brim and a red, white and blue outfit with red collar. It has one red hand and foot, and one blue hand and foot. It stands on a blue base. Original retail price $45.